The AA 100 Best Walks in
Northern England

Produced by AA Publishing
© Automobile Association Developments
Limited 2004

Published by AA Publishing (a trading name
of Automobile Association Developments
Limited, whose registered office is
Millstream, Maidenhead, Windsor,
SL4 5GD; registered number 1878835)

Ordnance Survey® This product includes
mapping data licensed
from Ordnance Survey® with the permission
of the Controller of Her Majesty's Stationery
Office.
© Crown copyright 2004. All rights reserved.
Licence number 399221

ISBN 0 7495 4050 8
A01957

A CIP catalogue record for this book is
available from the British Library.

Please write to:
AA Publishing, FH16, Fanum House,
Basing View, Basingstoke RG21 4EA

We have taken all reasonable steps to
ensure that these walks are safe and
achievable by walkers with a realistic level of
fitness. However, all outdoor activities involve
a degree of risk and the publishers accept
no responsibility for any injuries caused to
readers whilst following these walks. For
more advice on using this book see page 13
and walking safely see page 64. The mileage
range shown on the front cover is for
guidance only – some walks may exceed or
be less than these distances.

These routes appear in the *AA Local Walks*
series and *1001 Walks in Britain*.

Visit AA Publishing at **www.theAA.com**

Colour reproduction by:
Keene Group, Andover
Printed and bound by:
Oriental Press, Dubai

Acknowledgements

Written and researched by Jon Sparks,
John Morrison, Andrew McCloy, John
Gillham, Hugh Taylor, Moira McCrossan,
Dennis Kelsall, Anthony Toole, David
Winpenny, Chris Bagshaw, Sheila Bowker,
Bill Birkett, Paddy Dillon and Terry Marsh

Picture credits

All images are held in the Automobile
Association's own photo library (AA World
Travel Library) and were taken by the
following photographers:
Front cover S Day; 3 A J Hopkins;
4/5 D Tarn; 6/7 E A Bowness; 8/9 T Mackie;
10tr C Lees; 10br M Birkitt;
11tl A J Hopkins; 11tr AA; 11br D Tarn;
12tl E A Bowness; 12tr S Day; 12bl C Lees;
13 D Forss.

*Opposite: Win Hill, near Hope,
Derbyshire
Page 4: Cow and Calf Rocks, on
the edge of Ilkley Moor, North
Yorkshire*

Contents

The Langdale Pikes rise above the village of Elterwater

Northern England

This is a region of great industrial towns and cities, high moors and mountains, lakes and beautiful dales, and sweeping sands and wild shores. There is plenty of history, too, from the industry that shaped so much of the landscape to the great castles and monasteries that came before.

Scots Pines reflected in the still waters of Buttermere in the Lake District

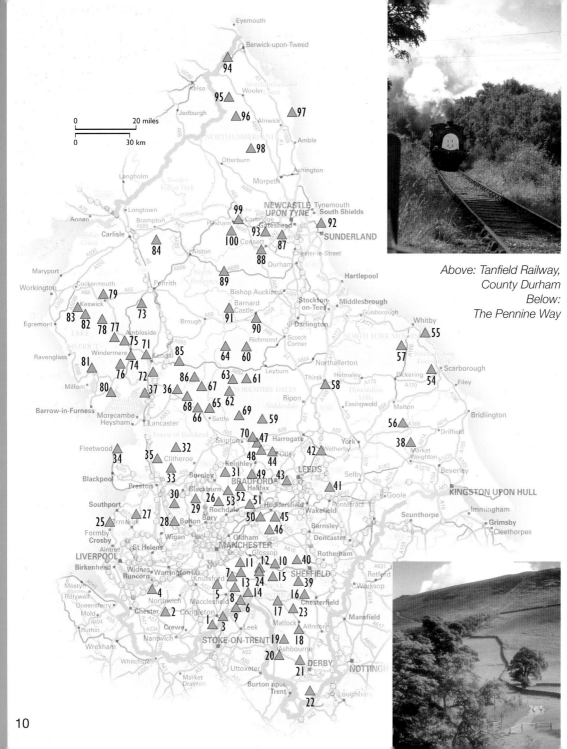

Northern England

This is walking country, which boasts five national parks: the Peak District, the Lake District, the North York Moors, the Yorkshire Dales and the Northumberland National Park. And down the centre, from Derbyshire to Scotland, runs the 256-mile (412km) Pennine Way.

From the Peak District National Park to the Lake District and the Scottish border, the northwest of England has mountains, lakes, and beautiful dales for the walker to discover. There are also lesser-known gems here – the high grouse moors of Bowland, the magical meandering Eden Valley, but this is also a region of historic cities – from ancient Chester to the Beatles' Liverpool. The hills dominate the northeast. The gritstone Pennines form a western boundary, only broken where the Tyne breaks through against the Scottish border. But there is also excellent walking along Yorkshire's heritage coast and on the wild Northumbrian shore.

Above: Tanfield Railway, County Durham
Below: The Pennine Way

Bowland and the Cheshire Plain

Bowland Forest is a huge empty space of high moors and remote valleys. Below it the Lancashire plain is squeezed towards the sea. The Arnside and Silverdale Area of Outstanding Natural

Edale in the Peak District is at the start of the Pennine Way

Beauty packs in a great deal of habitat diversity between the rivers Keer and Kent.

White Peak and Dark Peak
The White Peak is a limestone warren of dales and pretty stone villages and we have included walks around Ashford-in-the-Water and Tissington, which has a tradition of well-dressing. In the hills, you'll find nearly every valley has been flooded to quench the ceaseless metropolitan demand for water, which has created superb scenery. Hayfield and Ladybower are fine stretches of water surrounded by craggy hills.

Edale is the centrepiece of Derbyshire's Dark Peak. The pioneers of rambling started out from Chinley and Hayfield in the 1930s. And from Edale, the Pennine Way National Trail, the first long-distance footpath in Britain, begins its boggy journey northwards.

East of the Pennines
On the eastern slopes of the Pennines, West Yorkshire's towns and cities spill out over the eastern plains. To the south, Sheffield bites a share of this upland scenery, the millstone edges overlooking Derbyshire's dales. Yorkshire claims the lion's share of the Pennines. Here you will find the Three Peaks – Pen-y-ghent, Ingleborough and Whernside, as well as the Dales – Wharfedale, Swaledale, Wensleydale and a host of other valleys.

Moors and Hills
East of the Dales, across the Plain of York, the North York Moors and Howardian Hills rise up to meet the North Sea coast. The heather-topped moors seem to stop abruptly at the ocean – diving down in precipitous cliffs. Beyond these, and the great Tees river, industry has taken its toll.

Grey stone cottages in village of Muker, the Yorkshire Dales

But at Marsden Bay there is unsurpassed coastal scenery, then the Northumbrian coastline of beaches, dunes, castles and quiet inlets.

Lead mining dominated the North Pennines dales and the remains can be seen as you follow the rivers into Northumberland. Across the Tyne, and the Roman wall, the Cheviot Hills form an effective barrier against the Scots, and west of here the Border forest stretches into Cumbria.

Pennine Valleys
Bradfield is typical of many Pennine valleys – some have recovered better than others from the effects of industry. Striding across Rishworth Moor on the ancient trade route over Blackstone Edge you will feel remote. At Lydgate, ancient trackways take you high above the townscapes, and the sloping

Wades Causeway, near Goathland North Yorkshire

streets of Holmfirth will need no introduction to lovers of *Last of the Summer Wine*. From Wetherby to Addingham, there are many peaceful stretches of the River Wharfe to explore. Rising above, the slopes of Ilkley Moor inspired a Yorkshire anthem.

Stock Ghyll Force at Ambleside in the Lake District

The Yorkshire Dales

The Yorkshire Dales proper start north of Ilkley and Skipton. The sight of Bolton Abbey's priory ruins by the River Wharfe will persuade you that you have left the cities behind. Nidderdale has reservoirs and limestone scenery, as well as the relics of lead mining, high on Greenhow Hill. The limestone theme is strongest in the western dales and the waterfalls at Ingleton. North, at Ribblehead, you can see how the railway age tried to tame the wild landscape. The northern dales – Swaledale and Wensleydale – capture a special place in the hearts of all who visit them. The tiny village of Keld huddles on a hillside above the raging River Swale. Where the dale spills out into the Plain of York, Richmond and its castle stand guard. The River Ure runs through Wensleydale, an altogether more gentle affair.

The Lake District

The Lake District draws walkers and trippers alike for its sublime scenery. Windermere is England's largest lake, Wastwater its deepest. Scafell Pike is its highest mountain, Scale Force its tallest waterfall. The tourists flock to Coniston, Bowness and Keswick, but you can escape the crowds when you head further into the hills and dales. East of the Lakes, the River Eden has its origins high in the Yorkshire Dales, before winding beneath the highest of the Pennine fells to Carlisle, the Solway Firth and the border with Scotland. But those who make the journey over the Hartside Pass will be rewarded with a quiet, upland experience far removed from the bustle of Dovedale or Tarn Hows.

To the Roman Wall

Weardale and the Derwent Valley have been heavily industrialised, but now forests clothe their lower

Elterwater lies at the foot of Great Langdale in the Lake District

reaches, in a tangle of river gorges and industrial archaeology. If continue north you will come to Hadrian's Wall on the northern side of the Tyne Valley, now connected by a fine National Trail. And while you're here, don't forget to visit the attractive towns of Hexham, with its great abbey church, and Morpeth with its unassuming river and grand 15th-century castle.

Northern National Park

Beyond the wall you are in the Northumberland National Park, a sparsely populated upland corner that stretches to the Cheviot Hills. Here you can explore the remote valleys of the upper Coquet and the Rede, the Breamish and the Till. On the northeast coast the great cliffs of Marsden Bay are worth exploring for and no walker should forgo the opportunity to wander around Lindisfarne.

Lindisfarne Castle on Holy Island is reached by a causeway

Using this Book

❶ Information panels
Information panels show the total distance and total amount of ascent (that is how much ascent you will accumulate throughout the walk). An indication of the gradient you will encounter is shown by the rating 0–3. Zero indicates fairly flat ground and 3 indicates undulating terrain with several very steep slopes.

❷ Minimum time
The minimum time suggested is for approximate guidance only. It assumes reasonably fit walkers and doesn't allow for stops.

❸ Start points
The start of each walk is given as a six-figure grid reference prefixed by two letters indicating which 100km square of the National Grid it refers to.

You'll find more information on grid references on most Ordnance Survey maps.

❹ Abbreviations
Walk directions use these abbreviations:
L – left
L–H – left-hand
R – right
R–H – right-hand
Names which appear on signposts are given in brackets, for example ('Bantam Beach').

❺ Suggested maps
Details of appropriate maps are given for each walk, and usually refer to 1:25,000 scale Ordnance Survey Explorer maps. We strongly recommend that you always take the appropriate OS map with you. Our hand-drawn maps are there to give you the route and do not

Walkers take a break by the pretty arched bridge spanning Wycoller Beck in Lancashire

show all the details or relief that you will need to navigate around the routes provided in this collection. You can purchase OS maps at all good bookshops, or by calling Stanfords on 020 7836 2260.

❻ Car parking
Many of the car parks suggested are public, but occasionally you may find you

have to park on the roadside or in a lay-by. Please be considerate when you leave your car, ensuring that access roads or gates are not blocked and that other vehicles can pass safely. Remember that pub car parks are private and should not be used unless you are visiting the pub or you have the landlord's permission to park there.

---

00 | **Location** Walk title

Country • Region

❶ 4½ miles (7.2km) 1hr 45min **Ascent:** 131ft (40m) ⚠
Paths: Cliff top, shingle beach, farm track and country lanes, 1 stile
❺ **Suggested map:** OS Explorer 231 Southwold & Bungay
❸ **Grid reference:** TM 522818
❻ **Parking:** On street near Covehithe church

See the effects of coastal erosion on a walk along a rapidly disappearing cliff top.

❶ Take tarmac lane from **St Andrew's Church** down towards sea to barrier ('Danger') and sign warning that there is no public right of way. Although this is strictly true, this is well-established and popular path stretching north towards Kessingland beach and you are likely to meet many other walkers. The warnings are serious but it is quite safe to walk here so long as you keep away from the cliff edge.

❷ Walk through gap to **R** of road barrier and continue towards cliffs. Turn **L** along wide farm track with pig farm to your **L**. Path follows cliff top then descends towards beach to enter **Benacre nature reserve**. On **L** is **Benacre Broad**, once an estuary, now a marshy lagoon. The shingle beach attracts little terns in spring and summer and you should keep to the path to avoid their nesting sites.

❸ Climb back on to cliffs at end of Benacre Broad. The way cuts through pine trees and bracken on

constantly changing path before running alongside field and swinging **R** to descend to beach level, where you take wide grass track on your **L** across dunes.

❹ At concrete track, with tower of Kessingland church in distance, turn **L** following waymarks of **Suffolk Coast and Heaths Path**. Cross stile and keep straight ahead, passing **Beach Farm** on **R**. Stay straight ahead for 1 mile (1.6km) on wide track between fields with views of Benacre church ahead.

❺ Go through white gates and turn **L** on to quiet country lane. Stay on lane for ³⁄₄ mile (1.2km) as it passes between hedges with arable farmland to either side and swings **L** at entrance to **Hall Farm**.

❻ When road bends **R**, turn **L** past gate with an English Nature 'No Entry' sign for cars. Stay on this permissive path as it swings **R** around meadow and continues into woodland of **Holly Grove**. Pass through another gate and turn **L** along road for ³⁄₄ mile (1.2km) back into **Covehithe**. Turn **L** at junction to return to **St Andrew's Church**.

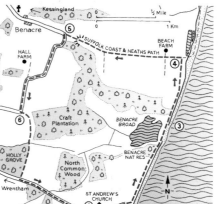

Map legend

← Walk route	P Car park
••••• Optional walk route	Cliff
– – – Adjoining footpath	Rock outcrop
–•–•– County boundary	Beach
Viewpoint	Woodland
▲ 392 Spot height	Parkland
Built-up area	† Church, cathedral, chapel
● Place of interest	WC Toilet
△ Steep section	⊼ Picnic area

13

1 Mow Cop Down and Up Again

5¼ miles (8.4km) 2hrs Ascent: 720ft (219m)

Paths: Open fields and woodland paths, canal tow path, quiet lanes, short sections where path indistinct, 10 stiles

Suggested map: OS Explorer 268 Wilmslow, Macclesfield & Congleton

Grid reference: SJ 857573

Parking: National Trust car park directly below Mow Cop castle

The lush plains and some wilder ridges.

❶ Head towards castle. Before reaching it take narrower path **L**, to road. Go **R**, then **L** ('Old Man' and 'South Cheshire Way'). Swing **L**, then **R**, then fork **R** on narrow path past Old Man. Rejoin wider track, heading towards communications mast.

❷ At junction of footpaths go **L**. Follow field edges downhill into wood. Where footpath splits at holly bushes go **L** and into field; bear **R**. Skirt farm then join rough track. Keep descending to join surfaced lane. Bear **L**; cross railway at Ackers Crossing.

❸ Follow lane to wider road and turn **R**. Cross canal bridge, then go down steps and **L**, along tow path. At bridge No 81 go up to lane and turn **L**, over bridge.

❹ Follow lane to crossroads by **Baytree Farm** and continue up track to **Limekiln Farm**. Take track on **L** just beyond buildings. Keep low, along edge of wood, until track bends **R** by post marked with yellow arrows.

❺ Go **L**, through undergrowth to duckboards and stile. Turn **R** along field edge. After 100yds (91m) there's another post. Descend sharp **R**; cross several, sometimes slippery, plank bridges. Narrow path heads uphill to wider track, then tarmac near house. Before track starts to descend, go **R** to stile. Follow **L** edge of field alongside wood. After another stile go up narrower field until it opens out. Above signpost, go **R** on green track to stile amid holly trees. Continue to another boundary; beyond is rougher ground with rushes and gorse. Firm track curves across this, though last bit to stile remains rough and rushy. Bear **L** up drive to road, then follow it **R** for 300yds (274m).

❻ By gateway on **R-H** side **Gritstone Trail** sign under tree points way into wood. Footpath roughly follows its upper margin and emerges on level floor of old quarry workings. Bear **L**, below communications **tower**, to rejoin outward route near **Old Man of Mow**.

2 Little Budworth Woods and Heaths

3½ miles (5.7km) 1hr 15min Ascent: 98ft (30m)

Paths: Easy tracks at first, field paths and some (usually quiet) road walking, 14 stiles

Suggested map: OS Explorer 267 Northwich & Delamere Forest

Grid reference: SJ 590654

Parking: Main car park for Little Budworth Country Park

An easy walk centred around the distinctive heathland of Little Budworth Country Park.

❶ Cross **Coach Road** to path; turn **R** on wider path. Fork **L**; follow main path, keeping ahead at crossroads, with Heathland Trail sign, and again at next crossing. When field appears ahead, follow path alongside to its **R**. This veers away **R**. Go back **L** just before cleared area, by Heathland Trail marker.

❷ Go **R** on track to **Coach Road** and over into **Beech Road**. After 230yds (210m) enter small car park. Go through gap in fence near far end beside signboard with map. Path skirts depression with boggy pool, then curves round larger pool.

❸ Cross causeway/dam by pool and gently climb sunken track beyond. As it levels out, fork **L** by Heathland Trail sign then **L**, with an open field not far away to **L**. Bear **L** on wider surfaced track, swinging down past ornamental pool in dip. Immediately after this turn **R** on sandy track.

❹ Where another path crosses, most people evidently go through gate ahead into corner of field. Strictly speaking, however, right of way goes over stile to its **R** then across (very wet and smelly) corner of wood to 2nd stile. From here bear **R** under power line, to stile in far corner. Follow narrow path (beware nettles), then go over stile on **R** and straight across large field. Aim just **L** of farm to gate and stile. Go **L** on lane for 60yds (55m) then **R** down track. This becomes narrower, then descends slightly.

❺ As track levels out, there's stile on R, with sign for **Budworth Mere**. Go down towards water then **L** on path skirting mere. At end go **R** up road, swinging further **R** into centre of **Little Budworth**.

❻ Keep straight on ahead along road, through village then past open fields. Opposite entrance gates of **Oulton Park** is start of **Coach Road**. Follow this road, or parallel footpath to its **L** for 125yds (114m), to car park at **Little Budworth Country Park**.

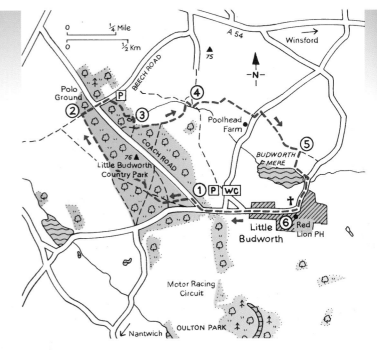

The Cloud Views from the Crest

7 miles (11.3km) 2hrs 30min Ascent: 804ft (245m) **2**
Paths: Field paths, canal tow path, some lanes, rougher and steeper on The Cloud, 11 stiles. Meadows and fields along canal, craggy summit
Suggested map: OS Explorer 268 Wilmslow, Macclesfield & Congleton
Grid reference: SJ 894627
Parking: Car park on outskirts of small village of Timbersbrook

An exhilarating walk to a superb viewpoint.

1 From car park, turn **R** on road for 500yds (457m). Just past houses, go **L** over stile and down track. After 600yds (549m) go **R** over stile. Follow trodden line to cross stream in dip. Continue diagonally across meadow. A short embankment leads to a canal bridge.

2 Cross and loop round **L**, under bridge and along tow path. Follow this for 3¼ miles (5.3km) to bridge 57. Go up steps and over bridge. Vague track bears **L** then **R** through gorse along edge of hollow. Descend to stile under sycamore then down slope (muddy) to footbridge. Cross stile, go down to **River Dane** and step round tree on its edge. Turn **R** up edge of field.

3 Cross stile to road. Turn **R** and climb steadily. As it levels out, go **L** on narrower lane. Opposite house, cross stile on **R**, then up fields over series of stiles, bearing slightly **L**. Join lane and go **L**, past **Hillside Farm**, then right, up track to stile.

4 Here is National Trust sign ('The Cloud'). Path is narrow but clear, directly uphill then slanting R. It passes below crags then levels out and dips slightly to start of broad shelf. Path now goes straight up hillside, through highest band of crags, to summit ridge. Trig point is about 100yds (91m) to **L**.

5 Retrace this short section of summit ridge then follow edge down, gently descending and swinging slowly **L**. Lower down path runs through pine plantations. Below gap in wall, broader track runs through more open woods. As track starts to curve **L**, clear path continues straight ahead. Stick to crest of ridge until you rejoin gravel track near sharp bend. Just below bend is footpath sign and steeply descending line of steps. Turn **L** on road, into edge of **Timbersbrook**. Just after 1st house on R go through gap in fence, down few more steps and across field with picnic tables. Car park is at its far end.

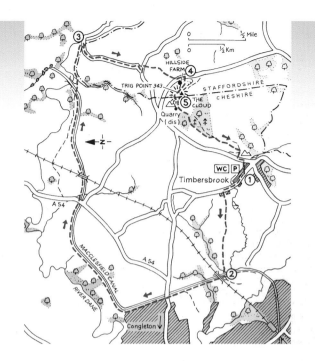

Frodsham Hill Sandstone Trails

3 miles (4.8km) 1hr Ascent: 375ft (114m) **2**
Paths: Clear woodland paths, golf course, 4 stiles
Suggested map: OS Explorer 267 Northwich & Delamere Forest
Grid reference: SJ 518766
Parking: Small car park on Beacon Hill, near Mersey View

A short walk on the crest and the flanks of a red sandstone escarpment.

1 Go **R** along lane for 100yds (91m), then **L** down sunken footpath and over stile to **golf course**. The path is much older than the golf course and officially walkers have priority, but don't take it for granted! Head straight across to 17th tee and arrow on post. Drop down slightly to **R**, crossing sandy patch, to footpath in trees **R** of green below. Bear **L** at sign for **Woodhouse Hill**, down steps. Keep to **L**, passing above crags; go down steps into **Dunsdale Hollow**.

2 Go **R**, rising gently, below more crags. Go past stile on **L** then up scratched steps on corner of rocks ahead. Follow level path through trees, near edge of golf course. Soon after this ends, path rises slightly and passes bench. After 20yds (18m), path forks. Keep straight on along level path, soon passing Woodland Trust sign, to wider clearing with signpost on **L** near corner of field beyond.

3 Just before corner of field, at break in overgrown old wall on **R**, narrow path slants steeply down slope. Bare rock on path can be slippery when wet, take care. Near bottom, path turns directly downhill to bottom corner of wood. Go **R** along base of hill. After 800yds (732m) path twists and descends into base of **Dunsdale Hollow**. Cross it and go up other side alongside stone wall and up steps. Go **R** on sandy track, climbing steadily and then passing below steep rock face.

4 Go **L** up steps, briefly rejoining outward route. **Jacob's Ladder** is just to **L** here, up R-H edge of crags. At top, bear **L** ('Mersey View'), and follow sandy track, with occasional Sandstone Trail markers, along brink of steeper slope. Pass below small steep crags before emerging near summit obelisk.

5 Turn **R** before **memorial** on footpath, aiming for telecommunications towers ahead. Go through ornate iron gates on to lane and turn **R**, back to car park.

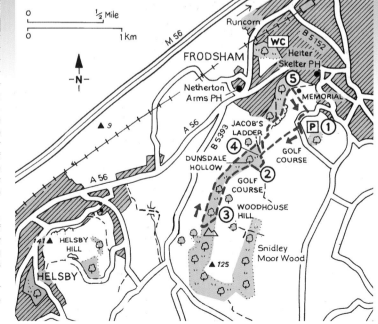

5 Alderley Edge Wizardly Wanderings

3 miles (4.8km) 1hr **Ascent:** 445ft (136m) ▲

Paths: Woodland tracks and paths, some field paths, 7 stiles

Suggested map: OS Explorer 268 Wilmslow, Macclesfield & Congleton

Grid reference: SJ 860772

Parking: Large National Trust car park off B5087

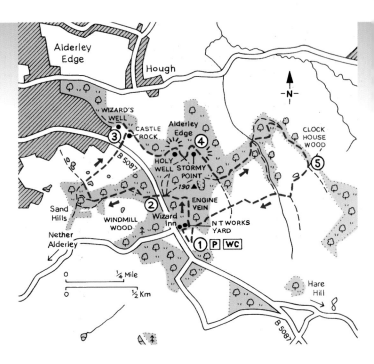

Layers of history and legend surround this famous Cheshire landmark.

❶ From large National Trust car park, off B5087, walk towards tea room and information room. Go **R** on wide track past **National Trust works yard**, then **L**. Cross open area past **Engine Vein**. At crossroads of paths turn **L** and come out by Beacon Lodge.

❷ Go straight across road into **Windmill Wood**. Follow descending track to clearing, bear **L** and continue. About 140yds (128m) beyond National Trust sign, in more open terrain, with bare sand hills ahead, bear **R** across grass to crossroads with field ahead. Turn **R**, skirting damp ground then pool. Just before another open field, go **R**, along edge of wood. Continue in strip of trees, with fields either side. Cross road again and follow track to crest of **Castle Rock**.

❸ Descend steps to level path. Go **L** 120yds (110m) to **Wizard's Well**. Return to steps and continue below crags on terrace path, then up steps to join higher

path. Go **L** and almost immediately start descending, with more steps in places. At bottom cross footbridge and climb, levelling out briefly by **Holy Well**. Few paces to **L** of well go up over tree roots to where path resumes. Climb shallow steps to wider path, go **L** then turn **R** on to crest of **Stormy Point**.

❹ Follow wide level track to crossroads; go **L**. Follow signs ('Hare Hill'), descend with small ravine at bottom. Turn **R** and ascend. Climb steps past beech trees, then descend through **Clock House Wood**. Climb again to National Trust sign and out into open.

❺ Go **R**, over stile, across waist of field to stile near pond. Go **L** along hedge to stile hidden in curve, then up fenced path. Join wider track and at top go over stile on **R**. Go **L** over next stile and up to stile and grassy track. Cross gravel track into narrow fenced path and at end turn **L**. Opposite **National Trust works yard** go **L** through gate for short cut to car park or continue straight on to tea room.

6 Shutlingsloe Mini Mountain

5 miles (8km) 2hrs **Ascent:** 1,129ft (344m) ▲

Paths: Farm and forest tracks, field paths, lane, moorland, 11 stiles

Suggested map: OS Explorer OL24 White Peak

Grid reference: SJ 984706

Parking: Car park at Vicarage Quarry, Wildboarclough (alternative at Clough House, lower down valley)

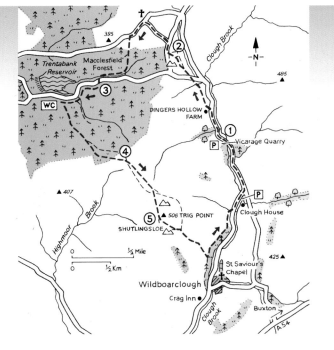

From valleys and forest to a stark peak.

❶ From car park at **Vicarage Quarry**, turn **L** up road, away from **Wildboarclough** village. Just past **Dingers Hollow Farm**, go over stile on **L** and up to iron gate. Go **R** through another gate and follow green track across hillside to 3rd gate. Cross field near power line, down to stream then up **L** to stile by gate. Cross lane and walk few paces to stile. Narrow path rises gently, but our route rises steeply, above large trees. Continue on this line to stile into another lane. Go **R** to junction.

❷ Turn **L**, on lane ('Macc Forest Chapel'), over top and down, past chapel. Follow road for 250yds (229m) to dip. At corner of wood go **L** on footpath, down hill. At bottom, near small dam, take newly made permissive footpath on **R**, over bridge. When gate blocks way, drop to **L**, down steps to stile and road.

❸ Cross to gap in wall almost opposite. Continuation path parallels road; when it rejoins it by gate, bear **L**

on wider path, swinging back **R**. Go up flight of steps on **L** and sharply back **L** on path climbing alongside stone wall. When gradient eases near kissing gate, bear **L** on established footpath. At next junction, after 300yds (274m), go **R**, with sign ('**Shutlingsloe**'), and up to kissing gate.

❹ Footpath, partly surfaced with large gritstone flags, crosses open moorland. At shoulder, path levels out and **Shutlingsloe** rears up ahead. Descend slightly, cross duckboards to stile and then follow obvious, flagged path alongside wall. Final steep staircase leads to trig point.

❺ Descend ahead, winding down steeply between low outcrops. Keep ahead as gradient eases. After 2 stiles follow wall to tarmac track. Go **R** on track to cattle grid. Take another track sharply back to **L**. This runs more or less level along hillside, then gently descending green track interrupted by stile and small stream leads down to road. Go **L** up this back to start.

Lyme Park Mr Darcy!

5½ miles (8.8km) 3hrs 30min **Ascent:** 950ft (290m)

Paths: Generally firm, field tracks can be slippery if wet, 12 stiles

Suggested map: OS Explorer OL1 Dark Peak

Grid reference: SJ 964823

Parking: Lyme Park, off A6 (free to National Trust members)

Around Lyme Park – Mr Darcy's home in the BBC's serialisation of *Pride and Prejudice.*

❶ With lake on R and house on L leave car park by drive and, as it begins to bend away to R, turn **L** for wide track through gate ('**Gritstone Trail**'). Follow through **Knightslow Wood**, negotiating several ladder stiles, until you reach moorland.

❷ Keep ahead/**L** on main track as it climbs moorland, aiming for small TV masts on skyline. At top, cross stile and field to reach end of surfaced lane by **Bow Stones**.

❸ Turn **L**; follow lane downhill until you reach junction, opposite hotel driveway. Turn **L**; walk up drive of **Cock Knoll Farm**. At buildings, head **R** across farmyard, following footpath signs. At far side go through gate and down **L-H** side of field.

❹ As you draw level with small thicket in shallow valley on L, go across stile and through trees. On other side head **R**, across bottom of field. Clear waymark

posts now point you through several rough fields to walled lane on far side.

❺ Once on lane, turn **R** and continue over **Bollinhurst Bridge**. (Turn **L** for short cut back to house via **East Lodge**.) Beyond Macclesfield Borough's newly planted Millennium Wood you reach junction of tracks. Go through gate on **L**; take grassy track, half **L**, signposted to North Lodge.

❻ Descend **R-H** side of field to woodlands at bottom. Path goes over several stiles as it skirts round **Bollinhurst Reservoir** – keep close to wall on L. Gated gravel path leads around side of Cockhead Farm, across another field and down grassy lane. At end of lane go **R** on to surfaced drive to **North Lodge**.

❼ Go through pedestrian gate at lodge; turn **L**. Walk along main drive for 250yds (229m). Take footpath up hillside on **L**, between short avenue of trees, to reach top of open, grassy ridge. Head for hilltop folly, '**The Cage**'. Continue straight on to return to car park.

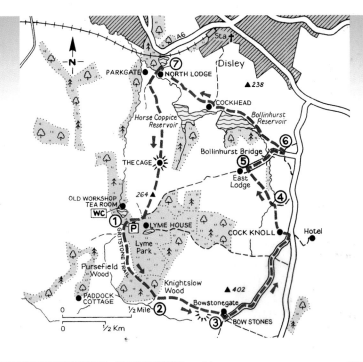

Bollington A Walk to White Nancy

3½ miles (5.7km) 2hrs **Ascent:** 1,180ft (360m)

Paths: Easy field paths and farm tracks, one short, sharp descent

Suggested map: OS Explorer OL24 White Peak

Grid reference: SJ 937775

Parking: Kerbside parking on Church Street or Lord Street, Bollington

A short but scenic ridge above Bollington.

❶ Walk starts towards top of Lord Street (which Church Street leads into) where it turns sharply **R** at top of steep hill. Walk along Cow Lane, cul-de-sac, then through gate at far end. Take upper of 2 field paths, quickly passing into larger sloping field on **R**. Aim for gate and cattle grid at far **L** top corner.

❷ Turn **L** on to open farm track; follow this all way down to lane in bottom of valley. Turn **R**, then almost immediately fork **R** again past some terraced cottages. Weir and pond below on your L are the remains of the former silk mill. Follow path through Woodland Trust's **Waulkmill Wood**.

❸ Leave wood via stile and go across lower part of sloping field, then in 2nd aim for buildings on far side. Follow gated path around to **R**, and on through successive fields.

❹ Go over stile with Gritstone Trail waymark (footprint with letter 'G') and along bottom edge of very

new, mixed plantation, then down walled track through woodland to reach main road at **Tower Hill**.

❺ Turn **R**; walk along pavement, past **Rising Sun Inn**, for ½ mile (800m). Turn **R** into **Lidgetts Lane** then as it bends almost immediately go **R** over high stile ahead and on to gated track, past row of hawthorn trees. Swinging **L**, follow grassy path up to ridge above – ignore lower route by R-H fence.

❻ Follow obvious hilltop track all way along spine of **Kerridge Hill**, ignoring tracks off L and R.

❼ Admire views at monument (**White Nancy**) at far end. This rather strange, bell-shaped monument was built in 1820 to commemorate the Battle of Waterloo – it was originally an open shelter but gradual decay and vandalism led to it being bricked up. Drop down sharply on to eroded path beyond, with **Bollington** spread out below; cross sunken farm lane and continue across 2 more steep fields to reach stile back into Cow Lane/Lord Street.

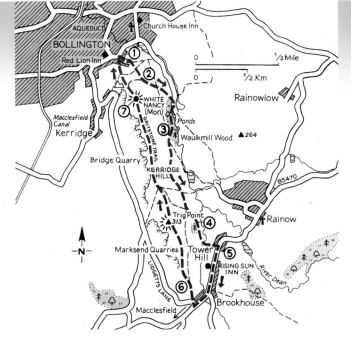

Cheshire • Northern England

Macclesfield Forest Royal Forest

7 miles (11.3km) 3hrs 30min **Ascent:** 2,820ft (860m) **3**
Paths: Sloping field paths, lanes and easy forest tracks, steep hillside, 20 stiles
Suggested map: OS Explorer OL24 White Peak
Grid reference: SJ 980681
Parking: Lay-by at Brookside, on lane 1 mile (1.6km) south of Wildboarclough

Another route around old and new Macclesfield Forest, then up Shutlingsloe.

❶ Walk along road for 440yds (402m) to **Crag Inn**, then at foot of its drive cross stile on **L** for path across sloping field. This maintains its direction through successive fields (each with ladder stile) until finally you reach farm drive at very top. Turn **L** and then walk along to bottom.

❷ Turn **R**; walk along lane as far as **Greenway Bridge**. Go over stile on **R**; follow path beside stream, until it crosses it to veer **L**, up **Oaken Clough**. Keep to bottom of little valley, past ruined stone shelter, and as it rises continue to its far head, near small **pond**. Turn **R** on to private drive; then go almost immediately **L** for wall-side path uphill.

❸ At top, go over stile and across moorland on clear grassy track. Keep ahead until you reach stile on far side. Cross, and descend sunken, fenced track to emerge opposite **Hanging Gate pub**.

❹ Turn **R**; follow road for 1 mile (1.6km), keeping ahead at junction where road bends sharply **L**. Ignore another turning on **L**, until finally lane turns **R**, into **Macclesfield Forest**, where there is wide gate on **R**.

❺ Don't go through main gate, but cross stile to **L** ('Shutlingsloe/Trentabank'); follow footpath, which runs parallel with lane. Drop down to newly planted area; cross footbridge; at junction of tracks, near wood sculpture, keep ahead ('Shutlingsloe'). At far end turn **R**, or for visitor **centre**/toilets at Trentabank turn **L**.

❻ Walk up wide forest drive; go **L** at fork; at far end turn **R** for long but quite easy gravel track through trees. At top go through gate, then continue ahead; turn **R** to leave forest for stone-flagged path across open moorland to distinctive top of **Shutlingsloe**.

❼ From summit descend eroded track down steep eastern slope of hill, until eventually turn **R** on to open farm drive. Follow this all the way down to road at bottom; turn **R** to return to car park.

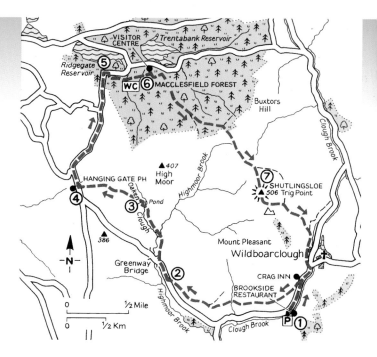

10 Ladybower Reservoir Lost Village

6 miles (9.7km) 4hrs **Ascent:** 1,200ft (365m) **2**
Paths: Well-defined moorland paths and a reservoir road
Suggested map: OS Outdoor Leisure 1 Dark Peak
Grid reference: SK 195864
Parking: Ladybower Reservoir pay car park

Beneath Ladybower Reservoir lies the remains of the old village of Ashopton.

❶ Turn **L** out of car park and follow road beneath **Rough Wood** and across Ashopton Viaduct.

❷ On other side, take 1st track on **L**, private road that zig-zags past few of **Ashopton's** remaining cottages.

❸ Where road ends at turning point, double back **L** on forestry track climbing through pines and larches. This track can be muddy after periods of heavy rain. Track emerges from shade of forest out on to **Lead Hill**, where **Ladybower Reservoir** and sombre sprawl of Bleaklow come into view.

❹ Path keeps intake wall to **L** as it rakes up bracken slopes of **Lead Hill**. However, at the time of writing, zig-zag path to **Whinstone Lee** Tor shown on OS maps has been replaced by well-worn path that diverts from wall to climb directly to summit rocks.

❺ Path continues along peaty ridge past **Hurkling**

Stones to summit. Beyond it meets signposted path heading from Ladybower over to Moscar. Descend **L** until you reach gate at edge of open hillside.

❻ Go through gate, then path descends westwards and alongside top wall of conifer plantation. It fords Grindle Clough's stream beyond another gate and turns **L** over stile to pass several stone-built barns. Path, now paved, descends further to join track running along east shores of **Ladybower Reservoir**.

❼ It's worth detouring to see **Derwent** village remains. It lies 400yds (366m) northeast along track at foot of Mill Brook clough. Afterwards, retrace your steps along well-graded track, heading southwards along shores of reservoir. After rounding **Grainfoot Clough** track passes beneath woodlands with rocks of **Whinstone Lee Tor** crowning hilltop.

❽ It meets outward route at gate above **Ashopton** viaduct. Turn **R** along road over viaduct and back to car park.

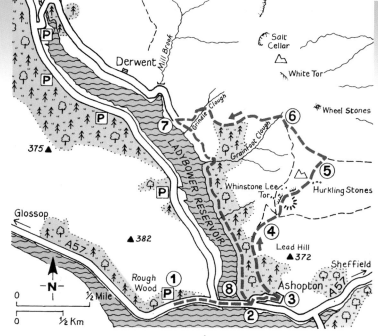

Hayfield On the Moorland's Edge

7 miles (11.3km) 4hrs Ascent: 1,640ft (500m) **2**
Paths: Good paths and tracks, plenty of stiles
Suggested map: OS Outdoor Leisure 1 Dark Peak
Grid reference: SK 036869
Parking: Sett Valley Trail pay car park, Hayfield

To Lantern Pike and Middle Moor.

1 Follow old railway trackbed ('The Sett Valley Trail') from western end of car park. It heads west down valley, above River Sett to meet A6015 New Mills road at **Birch Vale**.

2 Turn **R** along road, then **R** again along cobbled track behind cottages of Crescent into woods. Beyond gate, track meets tarred farm lane at hairpin bend. Follow higher course to reach country lane. Staggered to **R** across it, tarred bridleway climbs further up hillside. Take **L** fork near **Upper Cliffe Farm** to gate at edge of National Trust's **Lantern Pike** site.

3 Leave bridleway here; turn **L** along grassy wallside path climbing heather and bracken slopes to rock-fringed ridge. Turn **R**; climb airy crest to **Lantern Pike's** summit (topped by view indicator).

4 Path continues northwards from top of **Lantern Pike**, descending to gate at northern boundary of National Trust estate, where it rejoins track that you left earlier. Follow this across high pastures to 5-way footpath signpost to west of **Blackshaw Farm**.

5 Turn **L** along walled farm lane past **Bullshaw Farm**, then **R** on track passing **Matley-moor Farm** buildings. Where track swings **R** leave it for grassy track **L**. Cross stile at its end; continue northwards on grooved track, which joins surfaced track from Knarrs.

6 Turn **R** to **A624**. Cross with care; go over stile at far side. Turn immediately **R**, following faint track with wall on **R**. This crosses **Hollingworth Clough** on footbridge before climbing slopes of **Middle Moor**.

7 By white **shooting cabin**, turn **R** on stony **Snake Path**, which descends through heather, then kissing gate, across fields to reach stony walled track. Follow it down to Kinder Road near centre of **Hayfield**.

8 Turn **R** down lane, then **L** down steps to Church Street. Turn **L** to St Matthew's Church, then **R** down side street ('Sett Valley Trail'). This leads to busy main road. Cross with care back to car park.

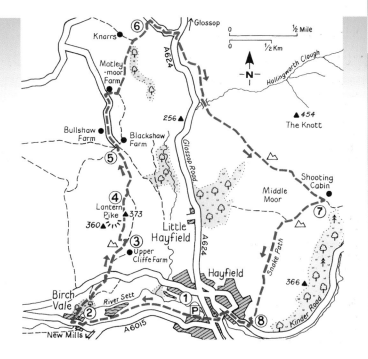

Edale Pennine Ways on Kinder Scout

5 miles (8km) 3hrs Ascent: 1,650ft (500m) **A**
Paths: Rock and peat paths
Suggested map: OS Outdoor Leisure 1 Dark Peak
Grid reference: SK 125853
Parking: Edale pay car park

A walk along a section of the Pennine Way as it ascends to the craggy outcrops of the Kinder Plateau.

1 Turn **R** out of car park and head north into Edale village, under railway and past **Old Nags Head** pub. Turn **R** by footpath signpost and follow path across footbridge over **Grinds Brook**.

2 Leave main **Grindsbrook Clough** path by side of small barn, taking **R** fork that climbs up lower hillslope to stile on edge of open country. Beyond stile, path zig-zags above Fred **Heardman's Plantation** then climbs up nose of **Nab** to skyline rocks. Where path divides, take **R** fork, which leads to summit of **Ringing Roger**.

3 Follow edge path **L**, rounding cavernous hollow of Grindsbrook past **Nether Tor**. Old Pennine Way route is met on east side, at place marked by large cairn.

4 Ignoring **L** fork heading for outlier of **Grindslow Knoll**, follow well-worn footpath westwards to head of another deep hollow, clough of **Crowden Brook**.

5 Cross over **Crowden Brook** and then leave edge to follow narrow level path traversing slopes on your **L** beneath imposing outcrop of **Crowden Tower**. This meets path from **Crowden Tower** before descending steep grassy hillslopes to banks of **Crowden Brook**. Path now follows brook, fording it on several occasions.

6 Go through gate at edge of open country, then cross over footbridge shaded by tall rowans to change to west bank. From here, path threads through woodland before descending in steps to road at **Upper Booth**. You now need to follow Pennine Way path back on to Edale.

7 Turn **L** along road and then **L** again into farmyard before crossing stile at top **R** corner. After following track to gateway, bear **L** uphill to reach stile by old barn. Here track traverses fields at foot of **Broadlee Bank** before joining tree-lined track into village. Turn **R** along road back to car park.

13 Chinley Edge of the Moors

5 miles (8km) 3hrs Ascent: 950ft (290m) 2
Paths: Field paths, quarry and farm tracks, a few stiles
Suggested map: OS Outdoor Leisure 1 Dark Peak
Grid reference: SK 041827
Parking: Roadside parking by Chinley War Memorial, Maynestone Road, or village car park

The green hills above Chinley.

1 From war memorial, head northeast up Maynestone Road. Leave it for signposted path (grid ref 042828) through narrow ginnel on **L**. Go over stile; climb northwest across fields towards **Cracken Edge**. At cart track turn **R**, then **L** on path passing between 2 hillside farmhouses. Go through gate, past farm on **R** before climbing to lower edge of quarry.

2 Swing **R** on sketchy path, passing hawthorn tree at base of hillslope. Join quarry track that zig-zags up slope before heading beneath quarry cliffs. Go over stile in fence over track; climb by this fence to clifftop.

3 Turn **R** along narrow edge path, then **R** again on grassy ramp bridging 2 quarried pits. Now descend **L** to prominent grassy track running beneath brow of hill and past **Whiterakes** cottage.

4 Turn **R** on track from **Hills Farm** then descend to tarred lane which passes **Peep-O-Day** to **A624**.

5 Turn **L** on pavement. After 150yds (137m) cart track (**R**) takes your route past quarry crater. Turn **R** at T-junction of tracks to traverse lower slopes of **Mount Famine** to reach col beneath **South Head** peak.

6 To detour to **South Head** take obvious route which leaves track to climb to summit. Back at col, go through gate by more easterly of 2 access notices. Go over stile by pole and descend southwestwards to walled track.

7 Follow this down to crossroads of routes north of **Andrews Farm**. Keep ahead into muddy field. Path soon develops into track and joins descending cart track from **Andrews Farm**.

8 On reaching **A624** turn **R** for 50yds (46m) then cross to signposted footpath, which cuts diagonally to **R** corner of 1st field before following wall towards **Otter Brook**. As old field boundary comes in from **R**, path turns half-**L** to cross brook on slabbed bridge.

9 Muddy path climbs out through scrubby woodland to **Maynestone Road**. Turn **L**; follow it to **Chinley**.

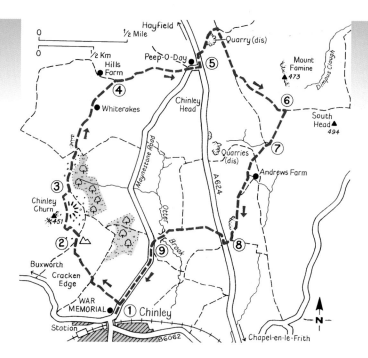

14 Goyt Valley Errwood Reservoir

3½ miles (5.7km) 2hrs 30min **Ascent:** 984ft (300m) 2
Paths: Good paths and tracks, a few stiles
Suggested map: OS Outdoor Leisure 24 White Peak
Grid reference: SK 012748
Parking: Errwood car park

Around Errwood Hall.

1 Take path signposted to **Stakeside** and the Cat and Fiddle pub, which begins from roadside just south of car park. Climb through copse of trees, go straight across cart track, then climb grassy spur separating **Shooter's Clough** and **Goyt Valley**.

2 Go through gate in wall that runs along spur; follow grassy path that zig-zags through pleasant woodland of **Shooter's Clough** before fording stream. Path heads north (**R**), threading through rhododendron bushes before continuing across fields to signposted junction of footpaths.

3 Turn **R** here on good path skirting near side of wooded knoll, then fork **L**, along path ('To Errwood Hall'). Path continues past ruins, and rounds other side of knoll before descending steps to ford stream.

4 Climb steps up far bank to reach another footpath signpost. Turn **L** along path ('Pym Chair'). This gradually swings north on hillslopes beneath **Foxlow Edge**. There is short detour down and **L** to see **Spanish Shrine** – built in memory of Dolores de Bergrin, a governess of the Grimshawes family.

5 Just before reaching road, path reaches more open moorland. Turn **R** along waymarked path ('2a') that climbs to top of **Foxlow Edge**. At old quarry workings near top, path is joined by tumbledown drystone wall. Keep to **L** of wall, except for one short stretch where path goes the other side to avoid crosswalls. Ignore waymark pointing into woods on **R**. That route isn't often used and is too rough. Instead, stay with ridge route keeping wall (**R**) and fence (**L**), which soon confines path as it descends to woods.

6 At fence corner, by woodland's edge, path becomes faint groove on grass slope. Follow it down for 100yds (91m) to where it meets narrow dirt path. Turn **L** along this, back into woodland, from where path descends to roadside at **Shooter's Clough Bridge** just 100yds (91m) north of car park.

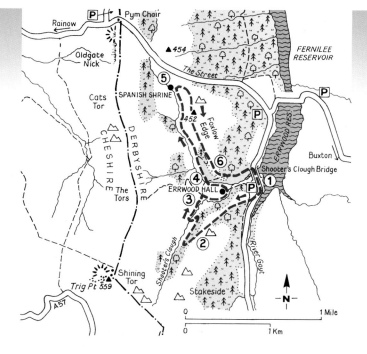

Hope Marching Roads

8¾ miles (14.1km) 5hrs Ascent: 1,050ft (320m)

Paths: Paths can be slippery after rain, quite a few stiles

Suggested map: OS Outdoor Leisure 1 Dark Peak

Grid reference: SK 149829

Parking: Main Castleton pay car park

Over Win Hill to the Roman Fort at Navio.

1 Turn **L** out of car park along main street. At far end of village turn **R** on walled lane; continue along well-defined path accompanying **Peakshole Water**. Cross railway with care; continue along path to its end at Pindale Road.

2 Turn **L**, then **R** at next junction. After about 100yds (91m), cross stile by gate; follow path running roughly parallel to lane at first, then **River Noe** to reach **Roman fort**. Beyond earthworks cross stile in fence; bear half **R** across field to reach **B6409** at **Brough**.

3 Turn **L** through village; cross footbridge. Go **L** over stile; head northwest to A625. Turn **L** along road for 200yds (183m) to small gate, just beyond cottage. Follow hedge and dyke on **R** to pass to **R** of houses.

4 Turn **L** towards railway station; go **R** along narrow path which leads to footbridge over line. Cross bridge; turn **R** at its far end, then **L** over stile to cross more fields, keeping fence on **R**.

5 At **Aston** turn **L**, then almost immediately turn **R** along narrow, surfaced lane ('To **Win Hill**').

6 Beyond **Edge Farm**, unsurfaced track on **L** leads along top edge of woods to path junction above **Twitchill Farm**. Now, climb **R** on well-used path to summit.

7 From summit retrace route back to junction above **Twitchill Farm**, but descend **L** past farm, to railway.

8 Turn **L** under tunnel, where lane doubles back **L** and winds its way to **Kilhill Bridge**, then **Edale Road**. Turn **R**, pass under railway bridge; turn **L** on field path.

9 By cottage turn **R** on path climbing towards **Lose Hill**. Take **L** fork at signposted junction of paths to follow waymarked route to **Spring House Farm**.

10 Beyond farmhouse, turn **R** on stony track heading west behind **Losehill Hall**. Where lane swings **L**, leave it; follow cross-field path, which joins unsurfaced lane. After passing outdoor activity centre, turn **L** along Hollowford Road, back into **Castleton**.

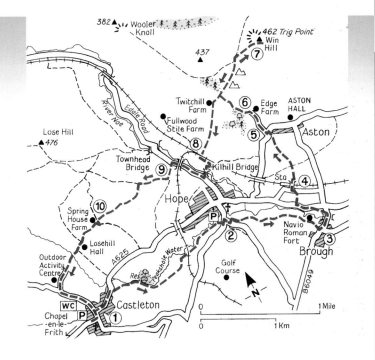

Chesterfield Linacre's Peaceful Retreat

5 miles (8km) 3hrs Ascent: 820ft (250m)

Paths: Generally good paths and farm lanes. Field paths can be muddy at times of high rainfall

Suggested map: OS Outdoor Leisure 24 White Peak

Grid reference: SK 336727

Parking: Linacre Woods car park

A walk around three reservoirs.

1 From bottom of lowest car park go down steps into woods. After about 100yds (91m) turn **R** along waymarked bridleway heading westwards, high above lower reservoir. Ignore path going off to **L**, which goes to dam of middle reservoir, but continue on wide bridleway along north shore of middle reservoir.

2 Take **R** fork on footpath raking up to top end of woods, high above upper reservoir's dam. Path continues westwards, dipping to one of reservoir's inlets. Cross bridge; follow well-defined concessionary footpath along shoreline.

3 At end of reservoir, ignore **L** turn over **Birley Brook**, but head west on waymarked footpath. Shortly exit wood via stile and enter first scrub woodland then fields with woods to **L** of wall and gorse bushes to **R**.

4 Cross stone slab across brook (grid ref 317727), then stile beyond it. Muddy path now climbs through more woods before emerging in fields north of **Wigley**

Hall Farm. It passes to **R** of farm to tarmac lane in **Wigley**. Follow lane to crossroads.

5 Turn **L** towards **Old Brampton**. Just beyond **Royal Oak** pub turn **R** down tarmac bridleway, **Bagthorpe Lane**, following it past **Bagthorpe Farm**. Lane, now unsurfaced, descends into valley of **River Hipper**, passing through farmyard of **Frith Hall**, down to river bridge. Winding surfaced track climbs to **Westwick Lane**, where you should turn **L**.

6 Just before **Broomhall Farm**, descend **L** on another track down to river, then up other side of valley into **Old Brampton**.

7 Turn **L** on lane, passing **George and Dragon** pub and **church**. Turn **R** by telephone box. Track descends to top edge of **Linacre Wood**, and swings **R**.

8 At junction of paths turn **L** through gate before descending to dam. At far side of dam turn **L** on metalled lane, passing toilets and ranger's office; climb back to car park.

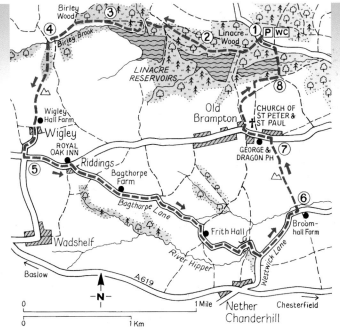

Ashford-in-the-Water The Valley of the Gods

5½ miles (8.8km) 3hrs 30min **Ascent:** 656ft (200m)

Paths: Well-defined paths and tracks throughout, lots of stiles
Suggested map: OS Outdoor Leisure 24 White Peak
Grid reference: SK 194696
Parking: Ashford-in-the-Water car park

Through lovely Monsal Dale.

1 From car park, turn **R** up Court Lane and **R** again along Vicarage Lane. Footpath on **L** ('To Monsal Dale') doubles back **L** then swings sharp **R** to proceed along ginnel behind houses. Beyond stile path enters field.

2 Head for stile in top **L** corner then veer slightly **R** to locate stile leading on to **Pennyunk Lane**. Walled stony track winds among high pastures. At its end, footpath signpost directs you **L** along field edge. In 400yds (366m) it joins track, heading north towards rim of **Monsal Dale**. Path runs along top edge of deep wooded dale to reach **Monsal Head** car park.

3 Take path marked **Monsal Trail** here – this way you get to walk across **viaduct**. On other side go through gate on **L**. Ignore path climbing west up hillside, but descend southwest on grassy path raking through scrub woods down into valley. This shouldn't be confused with steep eroded path plummeting straight down to foot of viaduct.

4 Now walk down valley. Right of way is well away from river at first but most walkers trace riverbank to emerge at **Lees Bottom** and roadside stile.

5 Cross A6 with care; go through White Lodge car park on other side to stile, where path back to Ashford begins. Paths are numbered here – this route uses number 3. Beyond another stile there's a path junction. Take **L** fork, which veers **L** across rough fields. Ignore next path into **Deepdale** and swing **L** (south) into **Great Shacklow Wood**.

6 Climb through trees and stony ground to footpath sign. Turn **L** here, following path ('Ashford and Sheldon'). After 200yds (183m) Sheldon path climbs **R**, but keep ahead, following ledge path along steep wooded slopes. Eventually path comes down to river, before joining minor road at bottom of **Kirkdale**.

7 Turn **L** along road to A6; turn **R** towards Ashford. Leave road to cross **Sheepwash Bridge**. Turn **R** on Church Street, then **L** on Court Lane to car park.

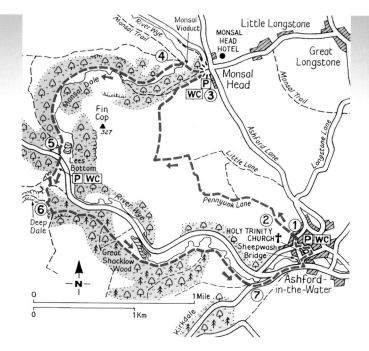

Cromford The Black Rocks

5 miles (8km) 3hrs **Ascent:** 720ft (220m)

Paths: Well-graded – canal towpaths, lanes, forest paths and a railway trackbed, quite a few stiles
Suggested map: OS Outdoor Leisure 24 White Peak
Grid reference: SK 300571
Parking: Cromford Wharf pay car park

Walking through a valley, which changed forever in the Industrial Revolution.

1 Turn **L** out of car park on to Mill Road. Cross A6 to Market Place. Turn **R** down Scarthin, passing Boat Inn and old millpond before doubling back **L** along Water Lane to Cromford Hill.

2 Turn **R**, past shops and Bell Inn, then turn **L** up Bedehouse Lane, which turns into narrow tarmac ginnel after rounding some almshouses (otherwise known as bedehouses).

3 At top of lane by street of 70s housing, signpost for **Black Rocks** points uphill. Path continues its climb southwards to meet lane. Turn **L** along winding lane, which soon divides. Take **R** fork, limestone track leads to stone-built house with woods behind. On reaching house, turn **R** through gate, and follow top field edge.

4 After climbing up steps, climb **L** through woods of **Dimons Dale** up to **Black Rocks** car park and picnic site. This track is former trackbed of **Cromford** and

High Peak Railway. Immediately opposite is there-and-back waymarked detour to rocks.

5 Returning to car park, turn **R** along **High Peak Trail**, which traverses hillside high above Cromford.

6 After about ¾ mile (1.2km) watch out for path on **R** leaving Trail for **Intake Lane**. At lane, turn **R** and follow it to sharp L-H bend. Here, keep ahead following path heading southeast along top edge of some woodland. (Note: neither path nor wood is shown on current OS Outdoor Leisure map.)

7 On nearing **Birchwood Farm**, watch out for 2 paths coming up from **L**. Take path descending more directly downhill (northwest, then north). At bottom of woods path swings **L** across fields, coming out to A6 road by **Oak Farm**.

8 Cross road and follow little ginnel opposite, over Matlock railway and **Cromford Canal**. Go past High Peak Junction information centre, and then turn **L** along canal towpath. Follow this back to car park.

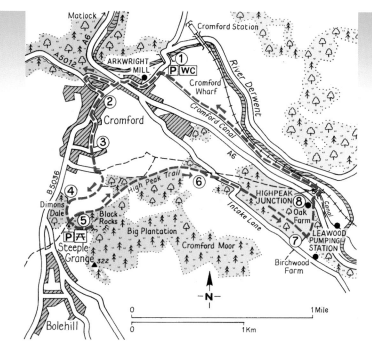

Tissington A Trail of Two Villages

4¼ miles (6.8km) 2hrs 30min **Ascent:** 525ft (160m)

Paths: Field paths, lanes and an old railway trackbed, lots of stiles

Suggested map: OS Outdoor Leisure 24 White Peak

Grid reference: SK 177522

Parking: The Tissington Trail pay car and coach park

Along a famous trackbed, the Tissington Trail, between two very different villages – Parwich and Tissington.

❶ From car park follow trackbed of northeast bound **Tissington Trail**. After 800yds (732m) leave trail and turn **R**, over bridge and along cart track.

❷ Just past 1st bend descend on waymarked but trackless path into valley of **Bletch Brook**, going through several stiles at field boundaries and across footbridge spanning brook itself. More definite path establishes itself on climb out of valley. It reaches top of pastured spur, well to R of small cottage.

❸ In next high field, path follows hedge on **L** to stile in field corner. It then descends to footpath signpost, which points short way across last field to western edge of village.

❹ To explore village of Parwich turn **R**, otherwise turn **L** down lane to Brook Close Farm. A signposted footpath on your **L** follows tractor tracks climbing to

ruined stone barn, beyond which lies stile into next field. Path now heads southwestwards to top R-H corner of field then follows muddy tree-lined track for few paces.

❺ On entering next field turn **L**. This first follows hedge on **L**, then descends to recross **Bletch Brook** footbridge. It climbs up middle not long field before zig-zagging up steep upper slopes to reach bridge over **Tissington Trail**. Go down to trail and follow it northwestwards through Crakelow cutting.

❻ After 500yds (457m) turn **L**, following Tissington footpath over stile to R-H corner of field. Now follow wall on R to **Rakes Lane** at edge of Tissington.

❼ Maintain your direction along lane to reach **Chapel Lane**. You can walk either way around village square. Hall and church are straight ahead, while Methodist **chapel** and **Coffin Well** are on Chapel Lane to L. Car park lies to southeast of square; take **L** turn just beyond **Coffin Well**.

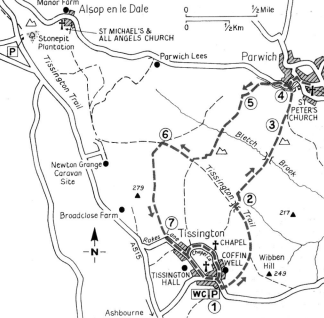

Osmaston Among the Aristocracy

4½ miles (7.2km) 4hrs **Ascent:** 295ft (90m)

Paths: Estate tracks and field paths, quite a few stiles

Suggested map: OS Explorer 259 Derby

Grid reference: SK 200435

Parking: Osmaston village hall car park

A gentle walk in aristocratic parklands.

❶ Turn **R** out of car park; follow road past **Shoulder of Mutton** to green and **duck pond**. Turn **L**. Take middle of 3 rights of way ('Bridleway to Shirley'). Wide track descends among fields and through woodland.

❷ Continue as track reaches beyond **Home Farm** (L), then follow it as it separates 2 narrow lakes.

❸ After water mill keep to track ahead, which climbs through woodlands of **Shirley Park**. Track eventually becomes tarmac lane, continuing towards **Shirley**.

❹ Return path to **Osmaston**, highlighted by **Centenary Way** (CW) waymarker, begins on **R**, just before village. Look around centre.

❺ Return to previous footpath, which begins in steps. Beyond stile, it crosses fenced-off section of lawn. Beyond 2nd stile, path follows hedge on **L** round edge of 3 fields. It cuts diagonally across 4th to stile; beyond turn **L** to descend towards wood, southern extremity of Shirley Park.

❻ Cross footbridge over **Shirley Brook**; follow muddy streamside path to another footbridge. Cross it then turn **R** into woods on path with CW marker.

❼ Beyond gate at edge of woods, ignore CW path on R. Instead, leave woods and follow sunken track heading west of northwest across fields and alongside lake, southernmost of **Osmaston Park** lakes.

❽ Where sunken track fades, keep ahead beside southern edge of narrow strip of woodland (valley of **Wyaston Brook**) and, although path is invisible, stiles in cross-fences are all in place.

❾ Bridleway from Wyaston Grove joins route just beyond one of these stiles (grid ref 196423). Double-back **R** along it, passing railings on R and entering woods. Bridleway track now climbs northeast out of valley and back into **Osmaston Park** estate. Follow it through park, ignoring private tracks to lodge. After passing through avenue of lime trees it emerges by village green. Turn **L** by **duck pond** then **R** to car park.

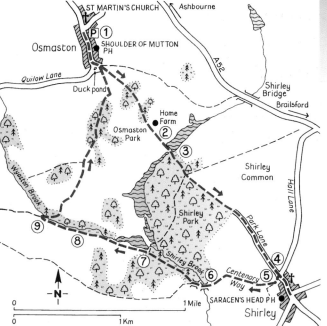

21 Mackworth A Rural Idyll

6 miles (9.7km) 4hrs Ascent: 197ft (60m)

Paths: Farm tracks and field paths (can be muddy after rain), quite a few stiles
Suggested map: OS Explorer 259 Derby
Grid reference: SK 333379
Parking: Markeaton Park car park

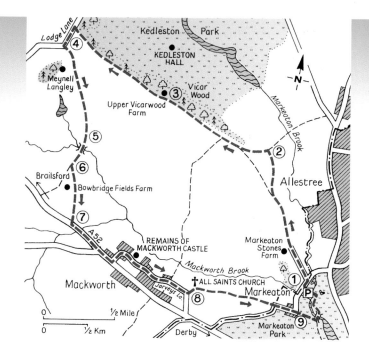

This slice of South Derbyshire belongs much more to the Midlands than the North.

❶ Leave car park at **Markeaton Park**; cross road to follow surfaced lane to **Markeaton Stones Farm**. Once past farm, track becomes stony, climbing gently up crop fields towards stand of trees on hilltop.

❷ At trees turn **L** at T-junction; follow crumbling tarmac lane alongside trees until you reach buildings of **Upper Vicarwood Farm**.

❸ At farm buildings continue through gate on L-H side of stable block; follow grassy hilltop track.

❹ Through gate, track reaches **Lodge Lane**. Turn **L** along lane to gardens of **Meynell Langley**, then **L** into field next to drive. Path heads southeast, following hedge on R. Through small, wooded enclosure lake appears in hollow to R. Beyond next stile, route enters large field and hedge wanders off to **R**.

❺ Aim for large lime tree at far side of field to locate next stile. Cross footbridge spanning **Mackworth Brook**. Path now goes parallel to hedge on **R**, aiming for large barn on hillside ahead.

❻ At gateway, path divides. Take path on **R**, whose direction is highlighted by waymarking arrow. Go through next gate; follow **R** field edge, passing to **L** of red-bricked **Bowbridge Fields Farm**. Now head south across fields following hedge on **L**.

❼ Cross stile in tall hedge; turn **L** along pavement of busy **A52** (take care), passing garage and Little Chef. After 600yds (549m) go **L** along **Jarveys Lane**, passing through **Mackworth** village.

❽ Where lane turns sharp **R**, leave it for path passing in front of **church**. Bonnie Prince Charlie waymarks show well-defined route eastwards across fields to **Markeaton**.

❾ At road you can either turn **L** to car park or continue through **Markeaton Park**. For latter go through gateway, turn **L** over twin-arched bridge, **L** by children's playground, and **L** again past boating lake.

22 Calke Abbey The House that Time Forgot

3¾ miles (6km) 2hrs Ascent: 197ft (60m)

Paths: Estate roads and field paths, a few stiles
Suggested map: OS Explorer 245 The National Forest
Grid reference: SK 352241
Parking: Village Hall car park, Ticknall

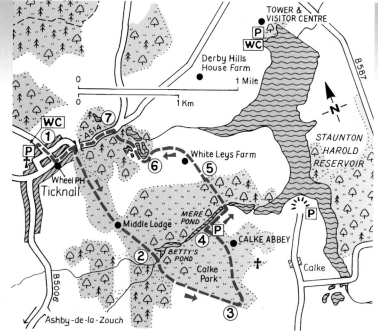

Around Sir John Harpur's forgotten baroque mansion, Calke Abbey, on Derbyshire's southern border.

❶ Turn **R** out of car park and follow road to its junction with A road through village. Turn **L** by **Wheel** public house, then **R** by bridge to go through gates **Calke Abbey** Estate. Tarmac estate road goes between avenue of mature lime trees and through **Middle Lodge Gates**. If you want to go inside **abbey** you'll have to pay here.

❷ Continue southeast along road, past **Betty's Pond** (L) then, as road swings L, carry on along grassy track that climbs to south end of park.

❸ Take **L** fork, which doubles back **L**, descending beneath hilltop church towards **abbey**, which appears in dip to R. After viewing fine house, continue along track past red-brick stables and offices. Cross car park and go through its exit on far **R**. Where exit road swings L, leave it and descend north, down to **Mere**

Pond, narrow strip of water surrounded by trees.

❹ Turn **R** along water's-edge path, then **L** between end of mere and western extremities of another one, to climb through woodland to north.

❺ On meeting lane at top edge of woodlands, turn **L** for few paces then **R** through gate. After tracing wall on L, go over stile in hedge ahead to enter next field. Path now heads north of northwest along **L** edge of crop fields, passing close to **White Leys Farm**. Just past large ash tree, go over stile on **L** and follow clear field edge track downhill through more crop-growing fields.

❻ On meeting flinted works road turn **L**, following it through area of woodland and old gravel pits (now transformed into pretty wildlife ponds). Winding track passes several cottages and meets **A514** about 500yds (457m) to east of village.

❼ Turn **L** along road through village, then **R** by side of **Wheel** pub to get back to car park.

Chatsworth Park and Gardens

7 miles (11.3km) 3hrs Ascent: 459ft (140m) ⚠

Paths: Good paths and forest trails
Suggested map: OS Explorer OL24 White Peak
Grid reference: SK 251699
Parking: Endsor village

Past gardens and through parkland created by gardening guru, 'Capability' Brown.

❶ From Edensor village cross **B6012**; take footpath at **R-H** side of large tree. Walk across parkland to join main drive to **Chatsworth House** near bridge. Cross over road; continue on footpath, walking downhill on other side to river bank.

❷ Follow **River Derwent** past couple of **weirs** and remains of old mill to next bridge that carries **B6012** over river. To **L** of bridge, metal kissing gate allows access to road. Cross bridge.

❸ Ignore **L** turn into drive past gatehouse to estate and take next **L** along side of gatehouse. Continue up hill, past house on **R** and then farm. Cross stile on **L** to footpath ('Robin Hood and Hunting Tower').

❹ Cross field and over next stile; go diagonally **L**, uphill following waymarkers on well-defined path. When this meets made-up track turn **L**, cross wall into estate by high stile and continue to crossroads.

❺ Keep ahead, following track as it passes **Swiss Lake** on R and then loops round **Emperor Lake** on L. Path will come to another, faint, crossroads. On L is **Hunting Tower**.

❻ Continue on path as it loops **L** around tower, ignoring turn off to R. Path heads downhill, past what appears to be remains of old viaduct with water cascading from end, then doubles back, still going downhill, eventually reaching car park at **Chatsworth House**.

❼ Go past wooden hut at car park entrance; turn **R** on to estate road heading north. Follow road past several wooden sculptures until you are within sight of gates at end of estate.

❽ Near here turn **L** across park to gate that leads eventually to **Baslow**. Don't go through gate but turn **L** on to trail that follows river back to Chatsworth. Turn **R** on to road, cross bridge then go immediately **R** on track, which leads back to **Edensor** village.

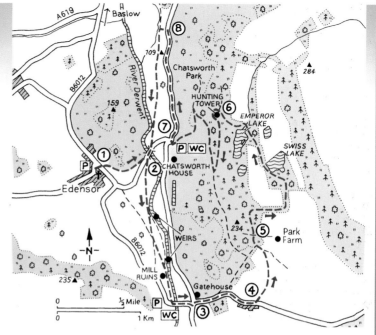

Edale Mysterious Mam Tor

6 miles (9.7km) 3hrs 30min Ascent: 984ft (300m) ⚠

Paths: Mainly good but can be boggy in wet weather
Suggested map: OS Explorer OL24 White Peak
Grid reference: SK 124853
Parking: Good public car park at Edale

Approaching from the Edale side, discover the ancient secrets of the great 'Shivering Mountain'.

❶ Exit car park at **Edale** and turn **R** on to road. Look out for public footpath sign on your **L** and turn on to farm road. Just before this road turns sharply L, take public footpath that forks off to **R** and goes uphill through wood.

❷ At end of wooded area, cross over stile and continue uphill. Cross another stile, follow path across open hillside and then cross yet another stile and turn **L** on to road. Just before road bends sharply L, cross over road, go over stile and then follow this path towards hill.

❸ Near foot of hill, cross over stile to **L** and then turn **R** on to road. Continue to find some steps on **L** leading through ramparts of Iron-Age fort to summit of **Mam Tor**, enjoy the views. From here retrace your steps back to road.

❹ Cross road, go over stile and continue on this footpath uphill and on to **Rushup Edge**. Follow this well-defined path along ridge, crossing 5 stiles. Where another path intersects, turn **R**. This is **Chapel Gate** track, badly eroded by off-road motorbikes. Go through kissing gate then head downhill.

❺ Near bottom of hill go through gap stile on **L**. Go across another stile, pass through gate, then across another stile on **L**. This leads to some tumbledown buildings. Cross over stile by corner of one building then veer **R** and cross another stile on to farm road.

❻ Cross road, go over stile and follow path until it joins road. Turn **R** then **L** at junction and continue towards **Barber Booth**. Take 2nd road on **L** then, near outskirts of village, go **L** on road ('Edale Station').

❼ Follow path across series of meadows, going through several gates and 3 stiles to join road to **Edale Station** next to **Champion House**. Turn **R** on to road then, near junction, turn **L** into car park.

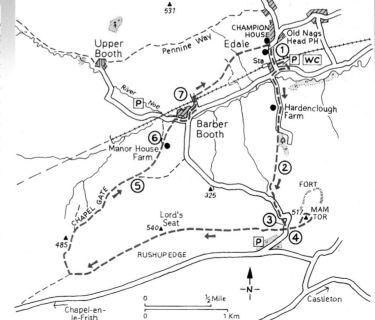

Formby Point Squirrels and Sand

3½ miles (5.7km) 1hr 30min **Ascent:** 50ft (15m) ⓐ
Paths: Well-worn paths through woods and salt marsh, plus long stretch of sand
Suggested map: OS Explorer 285 Southport & Chorley
Grid reference: SD 278082
Parking: Either side of access road just beyond kiosk

An exhilarating walk through an area of great significance for wildlife.

❶ Start just **L** of large notice-board. Follow 'Squirrel Walk', with its wooden fencing, to **L** and then round to **R**. Keep straight on at crossroads, where there's sign for **Blundell Avenue**. There are many subsidiary paths but the main line runs virtually straight ahead to **Blundell Avenue**. Cross avenue to fainter path almost opposite, with 'No Cycling' sign and traces of bricks in its surface. Follow this, skirting around edge of field (brick traces still useful guide). Go up slight rise then across more open sand hills to line of pines on rise ahead. Skirt **L** round hollow and see houses ahead.

❷ Just before houses turn **R** on straight track. This swings **L** slightly then forks. Go **R**, down steps, then straight on down side of reed-fringed pool. Beyond this keep fairly straight on, towards sand hills. When you reach them swing **L** then **R**, picking up boardwalk, to skirt highest dunes and out to beach.

❸ Turn **R** along open and virtually level sand. The firmest walking surface is usually some way out from the base of the dunes. Walk parallel to these (north) for over 1¼ miles (2km). The shoreline curves very gently to **R** but there are few distinctive landmarks apart from signs to various approach paths. Watch for sign for Gipsy Wood Path.

❹ Distinct track winds through sand hills then swings more decisively to **R** near **pools**, where there's sign board about natterjack toads. Follow track back into woods and, at junction, go **R**. The track curves round between woods and sand hills then joins wider track by Sefton Coastal Footpath sign. Go through patch of willows then bear **L** to line of pines on rise. From these drop down to broad path with gravelly surface and follow it **L** into woods again. Stay on main path, with timber edgings and white-topped posts, bear **R** by large 'xylophone', and it leads quickly back to the start.

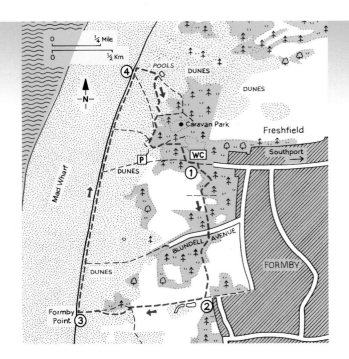

Healey Dell A Hidden Gem

2½ miles (4km) 4hrs **Ascent:** 640ft (195m) ⓑ
Paths: Field paths, old railway line and surfaced tracks, 5 stiles
Suggested map: OS Explorer OL21 South Pennines
Grid reference: SD 879155
Parking: Parking by Healey Dell Nature Reserve Visitor Centre

Around a gem of a nature reserve.

❶ With your back to **visitor centre**, turn **L** and walk past 1st range of buildings. Cross bridge; turn **R**. Take lower path, along river, past more overgrown ruins. Near green footbridge, go sharp **L** up bank then **R** along edge of clearing, and back into woods. Go **L** just before stream on narrow path, climbing steeply in places. Stone flags help you over wet patch before path dips to cross stream. Climb again on other side and join broader green track. Where this narrows, continue over stile and up edge of field to **Smallshaw Farm**.

❷ Go **L** before 1st building then through gate into yard. Go **L** on track to road. Go **R** and up to bus turning circle. Turn **R** opposite this, along track. Follow this for about 400yds (366m) to **Knack's Farm**.

❸ Continue over cattle grid and down lane between high banks, then fork **R** on track. After slight dog-leg track becomes greener. Follow it round **L** and back **R**, then over stile ahead and down field by ruined wall. Go

over stile at bottom, down to reach lane and then go **L** for a few paces.

❹ Go down ramp and steps to **old railway** line. Turn **R** along it for 500yds (457m), then cross viaduct high above **Healey Dell**. Go **L** down steps to access lane, down under viaduct then sharply back **R** on broad path. Where this starts to level out there is stile on **L**. But first go a short way upstream, until path starts to climb again, to see **cascades**.

❺ Return to stile and cross it. Follow stone setts (which are often slippery) down to sharp bend, with more remains just down and **R**. From bend, footpath follows tops of some old walls then curls down steeply to weir. Step across water-cut on stone slabs and follow it down. When it enters tunnel carved in solid rock, footpath goes to **R**. Almost opposite tall pillar it swings away from river and out past terrace of houses to lane. Go down this below to tall brick retaining wall and back to start at **visitor centre**.

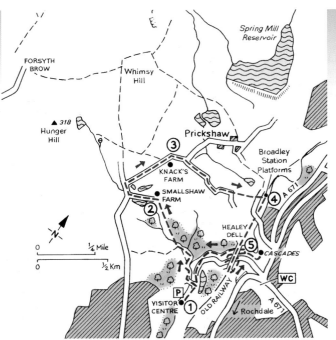

Martin Mere Lancashire's 'Fens'

5 miles (8km) 2hrs Ascent: 50ft (15m) 🅐
Paths: Canal tow paths, lanes, farm tracks and field paths, 2 stiles
Suggested map: OS Explorer 285 Southport & Chorley
Grid reference: SD 423126
Parking: Several small lay-bys near mid-point of Gorst Lane

An easy walk around a superb bird centre.

❶ Near mid-point of **Gorst Lane** at timber yard, follow short track via yard to meet canal by swing bridge. Go **R** along tow path for ¾ mile (1.2km) to **Gregson's Bridge**. Go under bridge then up to lane.
❷ Join wider road (Martin Lane) and follow it from canal for 350yds (320m). At bend, by **Martin Inn**, bear **R** down narrow lane. Follow this for 700yds (640m), past farm, to open section. Opposite glasshouses find footpath sign on **R**. Follow track to railway line.
❸ Cross line and descend track to green shed. Go **R**, alongside drainage ditch, to another ditch. Go **L**. Continue to stile by gate then go **R** alongside reed-lined channel. Follow over 2 bridges, 2nd bridge is close to corner of **Martin Mere Reserve**. Continue down green track, following edge of reserve, to road (**Tarlscough Lane**).
❹ Turn **R** and follow road for 500yds (457m). Immediately past **Brandreth Farm** find footpath sign.

Go down side of large shed, go **R** then **L** round pool and on down obvious track.
❺ At end, just before lane, turn **R** on track. Turn **R** before house and follow fence round to **L**. Keep almost straight on, past signpost, and follow footpath through crops towards 2 trees. These act as signposts down field edges to railway line. Cross and keep ahead, following slightly raised line of old field boundaries; join track to and through **Crabtree Bridge Farm**.
❻ Swing **R** on tow path and continue for 200yds (183m) to swing bridge by **Farmers Arms** pub and 500yds (457m) to smaller one above timber yard. Drop back down through this to **Gorst Lane**.
Important note: During bird migration season (1 Oct–1 Apr) avoid path immediately beside reserve and use alternative route: turn **R** just before 1st railway crossing (Point ❸). Walk alongside line to New Lane Station. Turn **L** up Marsh Moss Lane to junction with Tarlscough Lane and rejoin main route.

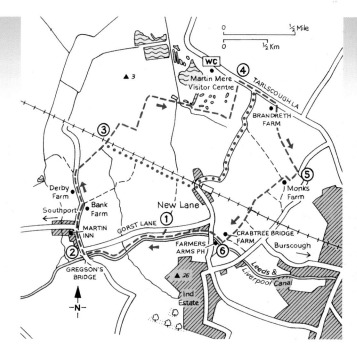

Anglezarke Rocks and Water

7 miles (11.3km) 2hrs 30min Ascent: 689ft (210m) 🅐
Paths: Mostly good tracks with some field paths, 20 stiles
Suggested map: OS Explorer 287 West Pennine Moors
Grid reference: SD 621161
Parking: Large car park at Anglezarke

Walking in a landscape shaped by reservoirs and quarries.

❶ Leave car park by kissing gate and follow track near water. Fork **R**, via Lester Mill **Quarry**; go **R**, and straight on at next junction. Track climbs steep rise.
❷ Go through gap on **L**, on bend. Path traverses wooded slope. Descend steps, join wider track and go **L**. Beyond stile follow narrower path to road.
❸ Go **L** 50yds (46m) to kissing gate. Follow track up valley below **Stronstrey Bank**. Cross bridge then go through kissing gate and over another bridge to **White Coppice** cricket ground.
❹ Bear **L** up lane, then follow tarmac into White Coppice hamlet. Cross bridge by post-box. Follow stream then go up **L** by reservoir. Bear **L** to stile. Cross next field to top **R** corner and go **R** on lane. Where it bends **R** go **L** up track.
❺ Skirt **Higher Healey**, follow field edges, then angle up **L** into dark plantations. Fork **L** just inside, and

ascend to an old **quarry**. Follow its rim for three-quarters of way round then bear away **L** through larch plantation.
❻ Go **L** on clear path then **R** to large cairn on **Grey Heights**. Descend slightly **R**, winding down past small plantation, and join wider green track. Bear **L** over small rise; follow track to lane by **White House** farm.
❼ Cross stile on **L**, below farmyard wall; bear **L** to corner of field. Cross stile on **L** then go up field edge and join confined path. From stile on **R** follow trees along field edge to rough track. Go **R** and ahead to **Kays Farm**.
❽ Go **R** down track then **L** on lane below reservoir wall. As lane angles away, go **L** over stile then skirt reservoir until pushed away from water by wood. Join road across dam. Go through gap and up steep track. Go **L** at top round **Yarrow Reservoir** to road.
❾ Go **L**, passing entrance to **Anglezarke Quarry**, to junction. Go **R**, and car park entrance is on 1st bend.

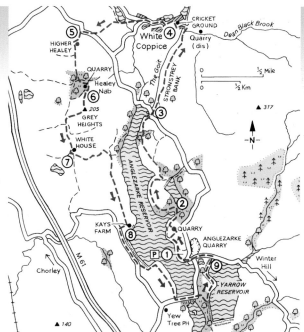

29

Haslingden Grane The Deserted Valley

3½ miles (5.7km) 1hrs 30min **Ascent:** 426ft (130m) 🔺3
Paths: Good tracks, a few steep and rough sections, 11 stiles
Suggested map: OS Explorer 287 West Pennine Moors
Grid reference: SD 750231
Parking: At Clough Head Information Centre, on A6177

A walk that lays bare the past.

❶ Footpath starts immediately **L** of information centre. Go through small plantation then climb alongside wall. Cross stile by **Rossendale Way** sign then go immediately **L** over stone slab stile and follow path along fine wall. After 100yds (91m) past plantation, go **L** over stile by **Rossendale Way** sign and down to road.

❷ Go **L** down road for 90yds (82m), then **R** on track, swinging **R** to pass ruins. After 440yds (402m) track swings **L** near spoil heaps. Keep ahead, past more ruins then dip into small valley beside old water-cut.

❸ Go **R** 50yds (46m) on walled track, then **L** again across short wet patch. Follow old walled track past ruined houses and into another small valley, just above extensive ruins. Skirt rightwards round these, descend to stream then climb up alongside plantation. Cross into this at stile. Path starts level but soon descends quite steeply, winding past Rossendale Way signs, to

meet clearer path just before footbridge at bottom.

❹ Cross bridge and go up steps then across hillside below beech wood. Cross another small stream, go up few paces then go **L** and follow path through pine plantation. Continue along bilberry-covered hillside above **Calf Hey Reservoir**, passing ruin on **L** and through dip with small stream. Another 90yds (82m) further, you'll see solitary, large sycamore tree.

❺ Cross stile just below tree then descend slightly **R** to stile by dam. Cross it and go up tarmac path past some valve gear to gate.

❻ Go through another gate on **R**, then through gap in wall and up path. This runs alongside road to car park. Where this path ends there's another up to **L**, ('**Clough Head**'). Go up this, meeting access road again, then continue up steps and through small plantation just below main road. Go **L** up road for 50yds (46m) then cross it by footpath sign to kissing gate opposite. Short footpath leads back to start.

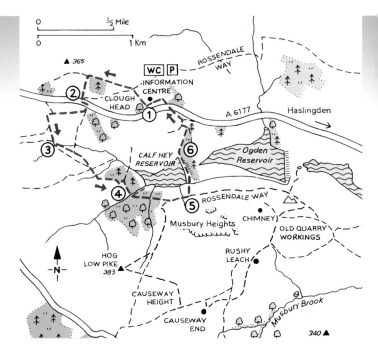

30

Darwen Tower Freedom of the Moors

4 miles (6.4km) 1hr 30min **Ascent:** 705ft (215m) 🔺3
Paths: Well-defined tracks throughout, 3 stiles
Suggested map: OS Explorer 287 West Pennine Moors
Grid reference: SD 665215
Parking: Car park near Royal Arms

A simple walk, if moderately steep in parts, to a great landmark on the moors.

❶ From car park cross bus turning area and then road. Go through gates and reach footpath sign in 30yds (27m). Go **R** ('Woods and Water Trail'). Path descends to crossroads. Turn **R** on broad path – still 'Woods and Water Trail' – then after 200yds (183m) go **R** at fork on gently rising path. Gradually curve to **R** and climb little more steeply, with open fields on **L**, out to road. Go **L** for 200yds (183m).

❷ Go **R** up walled track, part of **Witton Weavers' Way**. Go straight on at crossroads then descend steeply, with section of old paving, towards **Earnsdale Reservoir**. Cross dam and swing **L** at its end then follow lane up **R** until it swings **L** over cattle grid. Go straight up steep grass slope ahead, skirting fenced area with regenerating trees.

❸ Go **L** on track then, just above house, bear **R** up concrete track. At gap in aluminium barrier bear **L** on

level path towards old **quarry**. Here go up **R** on stony track then keep **L** where it forks. A gate on **L**, flanked by flagstones, gives a superb view of town of **Darwen**, dominated by the India Mill chimney. Continue along main track for another 100yds (91m). As gradient eases and **tower** comes into view bear **R**, past marker stone with its likeness of tower, and then go straight up to real thing.

❹ From tower bear **L** past **trig point** and the go along broad path above steeper slope that falls to **Sunnyhurst Hey Reservoir**. Path swings **L** past bench. Go over stile on **R** overlooking valley of **Stepback Brook** and down zig-zag path. Don't cross next stile but go back **L**, towards stream and then over stile at bottom. Go **L** on track to cross over stream.

❺ Track swings back **R** and up through wood. As it levels out pass to **R** of gates and continue down towards row of houses. Lane just **L** of these leads to road. Go back past bus turning area to car park.

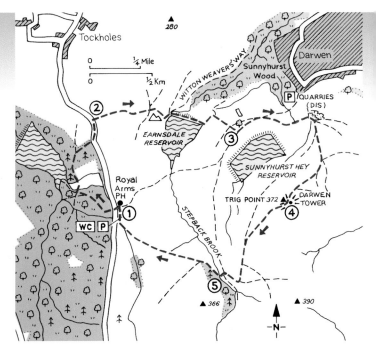

Wycoller Weaving Ways

5¼ miles (8.4km) 2hrs **Ascent:** 538ft (165m)

Paths: Field paths, some rough tracks and quiet lanes, 19 stiles
Suggested map: OS Explorer OL21 South Pennines
Grid reference: SD 926395
Parking: Car park just above Wycoller village (no general access for vehicles to village itself)

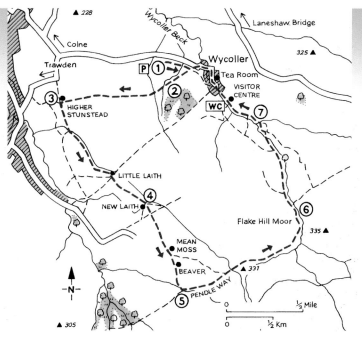

Around a district steeped in the history of the textile industry.

1 At top of car park are notice-board and sign 'Wycoller 500m'. Follow footpath indicated, just above road, until it joins it on bend. Cross stile on **R** and slant **R** across field to stile, then up to gate and into garden. Follow arrow through trees up **L** side to stile.

2 Bear **R**, cross stream, then bear **L**, up towards house on skyline, until footbridge and stile appear in dip. Follow hedge and then wall in same line. When it ends at open, rushy pasture bear slightly **R**, towards Pendle Hill. Cresting rise, see stile and signpost by corner of walls. Sign for Trawden points too far **R**. Aim slightly **L**, between 2 power line poles and again, once over rise, see stile and signpost by end of fine wall. Follow wall and then walled track to **Higher Stunstead**. Go past 1st buildings and into yard.

3 Go **L** up walled track to cattle grid then ahead to stile and follow course of stream up to **Little Laith**.

Continue to pass house on your **L** then go straight ahead, along field edges, to large barn on skyline by **New Laith**. Follow arrows round farm.

4 Continue virtually straight ahead to stile by gate and over more stiles to **Mean Moss**. Go few paces **L** up track then follow wall on **R** and more stiles to **Beaver**. Go slightly **R** down field to stile near corner then up by stream to track.

5 Go **L**, then keep straight on above wall following rougher continuation (**Pendle Way** sign). When wall turns sharp **L**, track bends more gradually, above stream, down to signpost.

6 Go slightly **L** to stile by gate then take lower path, down towards stream then up round wood. From kissing gate drop down to cross stream, then follow it down and out to lane.

7 Go **L** down lane to reach **visitor centre** and **Wycoller**. Go **L** up lane and join outward part of route back to car park.

Dunsop Bridge Moors at the Centre

9¼ miles (14.9km) 3hrs 30min **Ascent:** 1,247ft (380m)

Paths: Field paths, rougher moorland paths, surfaced road, 9 stiles
Suggested map: OS Explorer OL41 Forest of Bowland & Ribblesdale
Grid reference: SD 660501
Parking: Public car park at Dunsop Bridge

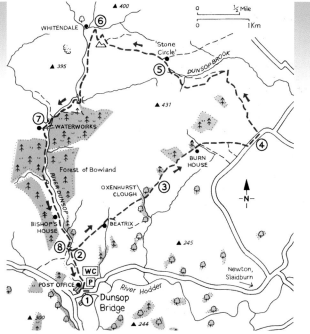

This is a tough walk on the high moors.

1 From car park, go up surfaced track, just to **L** of **post office** and tea room, for about 800yds (732m). At end of track, by houses, follow public footpath for 100yds (91m) then go **R**, up steep bank.

2 Cross large field, bearing slightly **L** to power lines. Continue to stile before **Beatrix** farm. Follow track round farm until it swings back **R** again. Go **L**, through 2nd of 2 gates. Climb slope **R** of stream, cross stile. Follow wire fence across hillside. Drop into **Oxenhurst Clough**; climb out through plantation, rejoining fence as gradient eases. Continue to join another track.

3 Follow track for ¾ mile (1.2km) to **Burn House**, where it swings **R**. Bear **L**, across open field, towards middle of young plantation. Follow path through it, bearing **R** to stile. Aim **R** of another young plantation in dip, then across field towards houses (Laythams). Go **L** on lane for 300yds (274m).

4 Turn **L** up metalled track. Clearly marked gates

guide you round house. About 50yds (46m) above this, drop to stream and continue up to its **L**. From top of enclosure, path rises to **R** alongside obvious groove, then swings back **L**. Climb ridge then swing **R** above upper reaches of **Dunsop Brook**. Cross plateau, parallel to old wall, to circular patch of stones.

5 Turn **L** and cross wall at stile. Path ahead is rough but clear. After slight rise descend, gently at first but gradually getting steeper. As ground steepens, descend in zig-zags, with gate halfway down. Just above farm at **Whitendale** go **L**.

6 Follow level track for ¾ mile (1.2km) until it swings round little side valley, over footbridges. Cross stile and wind down to track by river. Follow this down to bridge by **waterworks**.

7 Cross bridge, join road and follow it down valley for 1½ miles (2.4km), past **Bishop's House**.

8 Just after cattle grid, cross river on substantial footbridge. Just beyond this rejoin outward route.

Hurst Green Maybe Middle-Earth

6½ miles (10.4km) 2hrs **Ascent:** 459ft (14m)

Paths: Grassy riverside paths, woodland and farm tracks, 11 stiles

Suggested map: OS Explorer 287 West Pennine Moors

Grid reference: SD 684382

Parking: By Hurst Green village hall or on roadside adjacent

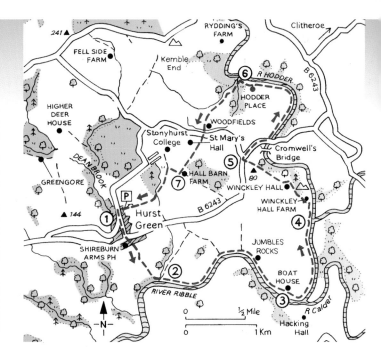

Did these rivers, fields and woods inspire Tolkien's creation of *The Shire*?

❶ Walk down road to centre of **Hurst Green** village. Cross main road and go down **L** of **Shireburn Arms** pub to stile below main car park. Go down edge of field then follow small stream to duckboards and footbridge. After slight rise, wooden steps wind down to **River Ribble**. Bear **L** just above river.

❷ Skirt aqueduct and return to river bank. Gravel track swings **R** past **Jumbles Rocks**. Go through gate alongside small stone building with mast to rejoin river bank and follow it, towards **Boat House**.

❸ After rounding big bend, go up slightly to track. Follow it for about ½ mile (800m). Opposite confluence of Ribble and Hodder, go over stile by bench.

❹ Narrow path quickly rejoins track. At **Winckley Hall** Farm go **L** to houses, **R** between barns then **L** past pond and out into lane. This climbs steeply then levels out, swinging **L** past **Winckley Hall**. Go through

kissing gate on **R** and across field to another. Keep straight on across large field, just **L** of wood, then down past pond and up to road.

❺ Turn **R** down pavement to river. Immediately before bridge, turn **L** along track. Follow river round, climb up past **Hodder Place** then descend again to bridge over stream.

❻ Go up track on **L**, cross footbridge then climb long flight of wooden steps. Follow top edge of plantation then cross stile into field. Keep to its edge and at end cross stile on to stony track. Keep **L**, past **Woodfields** and out to road. Go down track by post-box to **Hall Barn Farm** and along **R** side of buildings.

❼ Turn **R** on tarmac track for 200yds (183m). Go **L** through gate by end of wall and along narrow field. At its end go **R** to track alongside wood then up to kissing gate. Follow field edge to another kissing gate. At top of final field, through gate, narrow path leads to short lane. At its end turn **L** back to start.

Knott End Breezy Brine Fields

5½ miles (8.8km) 1hr 45min **Ascent:** 115ft (35m)

Paths: Quiet streets and lanes, farm tracks and sea wall, 3 stiles

Suggested map: OS Explorer 296 Lancaster, Morecambe & Fleetwood

Grid reference: SD 347485

Parking: Free car park by end of B5270 at Knott End

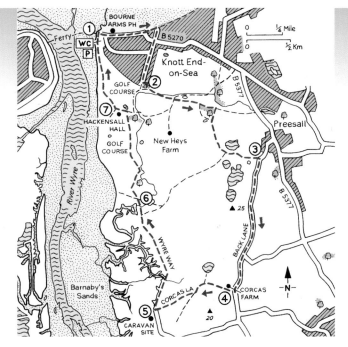

An easy walk exploring an unexpected corner of Lancashire's coastal plain.

❶ Go out to sea wall, turn **R** past ferry, along road past **Bourne Arms** and then along Esplanade. Where main road swings away, keep on along seafront, down private road then short stretch of footpath. Where this ends, before grassy stretch of seafront, go **R** down short side-street then straight across main road into Hackensall Road. Go down this almost to its end.

❷ Just before last house on **L** there's footpath (sign high up on lamppost) that wriggles round and then becomes clear straight track. Follow this through narrow belt of woodland, across open fields and then alongside wooded slope. Where wood ends go through iron kissing gate on **R** then up edge of wood and over stile into farmyard. Go straight through this and down stony track, which swings **L** between pools. It then becomes surfaced lane past some cottages.

❸ Join wider road (**Back Lane**) and go **R**. It

becomes narrow again. Follow this lane for about 1 mile (1.6km), over slight rise and down again, to **Corcas Farm**.

❹ Turn **R** on **Corcas Lane** ('Private Road Bridle Path Only'). Follow lane through brine fields. After ½ mile (800m) it swings **L** by caravan site.

❺ Go **R**, past **Wyre Way** sign and over stile on to embankment. Follow its winding course for 1 mile (1.6km) to stile with signpost just beyond.

❻ Go ahead on tractor track ('Public Footpath to **Hackensall Hall** 1m'). When it meets **golf course**, track first follows its **L** side then angles across – heed danger signs! Follow track to **R** of Hackensall Hall. Just past its main gates go **L** on track with Wyre Way sign. This skirts round behind outlying buildings.

❼ Path swings to **R** and then crosses **golf course** again. Aim for green shelter on skyline then bear **R** along edge of course. Skirt round white cottages, then go **L** to sea wall. Turn **R** along it back to car park.

Brock Bottom The Bottom and the Top

6 miles (9.7km) 2hrs **Ascent:** 689ft (210m)
Paths: Field paths, in places indistinct, clear tracks, 19 stiles
Suggested map: OS Explorer OL41 Forest of Bowland & Ribblesdale
Grid reference: SD 565426
Parking: By Beacon Fell visitor centre

Upland Lancashire countryside, by turns both expansive and intimate.

1 Look for public footpath sign in L-H corner of car park by **visitor centre**. Go down broad track, then through field. Bear **L** towards **Crombleholme Fold**. Walk, via farmyard, to country lane. Turn **R** to bend.

2 Go **L**, cross stream then up track swinging **R**. After 50yds (46m) go **L**, down to stile just before field ends. From stile, 15yds (14m) further on, go down field then angle **R** to low bridge and straight up track beyond.

3 Go through **Cross Keys** car park, through farmyard and into field. Go **R** to stile then straight on to corner of hedge. Follow it to tree then **L** to stile. Go **R** then straight ahead to lane and go **L**.

4 Go **R** to **Lower Trotter Hill**. Cross cattle grid, go **L**, then round to **R** and past house. Go through L-H gate and up to stile. Follow field edge, eventually bending **L**. Go down stony track and **R** on road.

5 As road bears **R** keep ahead. Descend on sunken track through woods; cross footbridge. Go up few paces then **R**. Follow path near river to **Brock Mill**.

6 Cross bridge then go through gateway on **L**. Bear **R** up track then go **R**, through rhododendrons. Follow edge of wood, then go **R**, crossing stream. Go up field edge and straight on towards **Lower Lickhurst**. Go round into drive and up to road. Go **L** few paces, then go **R**, up drive. Keep straight on as it bends **L**, up fields to lane. Go **R** for 140yds (128m).

7 Go **L** over stile and diagonally to isolated thorn tree. Continue to gateway and then to stile and footbridge. Follow old boundary, now muddy depression, then bear **L** to power lines. Follow these to marker post. Go **R**, directly uphill. Cross road to track rising through forest. At junction go **L** for 200m (183m) then **R** up narrow path to summit trig point.

8 Bear **R** along edge of forest then **L** across boardwalk. Keep straight on to **visitor centre**.

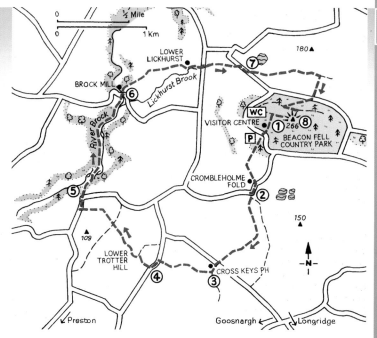

Leck Beck Over the Underground

7½ miles (12.1km) 3hrs **Ascent:** 968ft (295m)
Paths: Field paths, indefinite moorland paths, quiet road, 3 stiles
Suggested map: OS Explorer OL2 Yorkshire Dales – Southern & Western
Grid reference: SD 643767
Parking: Park by Leck church (honesty box)

The subterranean mysteries of limestone.

1 Turn **R** on road then **R** again. Turn **L** by post-box and go down lane, bearing **R** at bottom.

2 At end of tarmac take lower **L** track to stile then continue on good tractor track. Just after crossing stream track divides. Go **L** through gate into wood then continue through pasture, passing wooden house. Cross stile at end. Descend almost to river level then climb away.

3 Climb steeply for 300yds (274m) then go **L** in slight dip past ruins of **Anneside**. Path, now sheep track, runs level and straight to ruined wall. Cross dip of small stream then bear **L** out of it, crossing damp ground on to grassy shoulder. Follow crest of steeper slopes dropping towards beck to tree-filled gorge.

4 Go ahead on narrow path across slope – not difficult, but don't slip. Continue to upper reaches of **Easegill Kirk**. Look around, then retrace to crossroads and descend to level area below small outcrops. Cross

steep grass slope into gorge. After exploring this return to crossroads.

5 Take uphill footpath. Where it levels go sharp **R** on narrow track to ruined wall. Follow this up to **L** then along, above rocky outcrops to green conical pit. Continue up and to **R**, on sheep tracks, to long, straight, dry-stone wall. Follow this up to **L** to clearer path. Fenced holes now appear in shallow dip in moor. Bear **L** to nearest, then follow narrow footpath past 2nd and 3rd. Follow shallow valley with no permanent stream, past small sink holes to deep shaft (**Rumbling Hole**).

6 Turn **R** on faint footpath across level moorland to 2nd fenced hole, 200yds (183m) away (**Short Drop Cave**). From this head back towards dry-stone wall and, just before it, head up to **L** to road. Turn **R**. After 150yds (137m) **Lost John's Cave** can be seen to **L**.

7 Continue down road for 2½ miles (4km) to **Leck**. Turn **L** near church to return to start of walk.

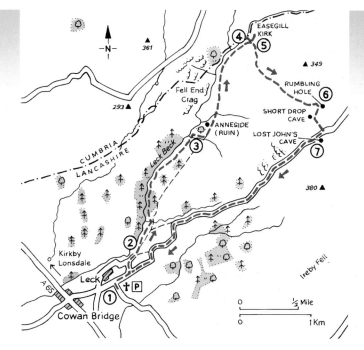

37 Silverdale A Quart in a Pint Pot

5½ miles (8.8km) 2hrs **Ascent: 426ft (130m)**
Paths: Little bit of everything, 10 stiles
Suggested map: OS Explorer OL7 The English Lakes (SE)
Grid reference: SD 471759
Parking: Small National Trust car park for Eaves Wood

Enjoy continuous changes of scenery.

❶ From end of National Trust car park at **Eaves Wood**, follow footpath to T-junction. Go **R** few paces then **L**, climbing gently. Keep **L** to beech ring, then straight on. Descend through complex junction to high wall and continue on this line to lane.

❷ Cross on to track ('Cove Road'). Keep ahead down narrow path (Wallings Lane), drive, another track and another narrow path to wider road. After 200yds (183m) go **L** down Cove Road.

❸ From Cove walk **L**, below cliffs, to shore. Walk up road to Beach Garage then take footpath alongside.

❹ At next road turn **R** for 600yds (549m) then bear **R** down Gibraltar Lane for 350yds (320m). Enter National Trust property of **Jack Scout**.

❺ Descend **L** to limekiln then follow narrowing path directly away from it. This swings **L** above steep drop and descends. Follow broad green path to gate. After 100yds (91m), another gate leads into lane. At end

bear **L** below **Brown's Houses**. Follow edge of salt marsh to stile, go up slightly, then along to signpost.

❻ Turn **L**. Climb steeply to awkward squeeze stile. Gradient eases, over rock and through lightly wooded area into open. Go **L** to stile; follow wall down and into small wood. Follow track down **R**. Cross road to gap in wall, descend then walk below crags to **Woodwell**.

❼ Path ('The Green via cliff path') leads to rocky staircase. At top go ahead to join broader path. Follow it **L**, slant **R**; continue into woodland. Stile on **R** and narrow section lead to road. Go **R** 100yds (91m), then **L** into The Green. Keep **R** at junction; join wider road.

❽ Go **L** for 75yds (69m) then **R** ('Burton Well Lambert's Meadow'). Track soon descends then swings **L**, passing Burton Well on **R**. Cross stile into **Lambert's Meadow**, then go **R**, over footbridge to gate. Climb up, with steps, and continue more easily to fork. Go **L** alongside pool (**Bank Well**) into lane. Go **L** and at end car park is virtually opposite.

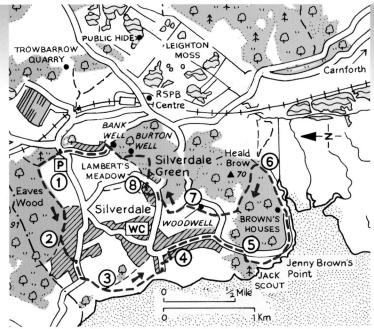

38 Huggate Fridaythorpe

6½ miles (10.4km) 3hrs **Ascent: 738ft (225m)**
Paths: Field path, farm tracks, 1 stile
Suggested map: OS Explorer 294 Market Weighton & Yorkshire Wolds Central
Grid reference: SE 882551
Parking: On street around village green

Open fields and hidden dales.

❶ From green, walk past play area and duck pond. Continue past cottages to junction. Turn **R**, down lane. Past last house, fork **L** ('Wolds Way'). Follow access road for ½ mile (800m) until it bends **R** into farmyard. Take path **L** between fences. Emerge on road on other side of farm. Continue up to fingerpost on horizon.

❷ Turn **R** along field-edge path ('Chalkland Way'). At end of field, go through gate and turn **L** along top of **Horse Dale**. Track descends to valley floor and gate. Go through gate and up side valley. Aim for R-H fence corner and go through L-H gate. Continue up enclosed track ignoring gate to R. After 300yds (274m) track continues along edge of open field. Eventually reach crossing track to **Wold House Farm**.

❸ Turn **R** along track into farmyard. Bear **L** along yard, through gate diagonally opposite. Bear **R**; continue on track across 3 fields. At end of 3rd field, turn **L** (don't follow right of way); turn **R** down side of

field to gate. Bear **L** with rising track above **Holm Dale**; then dip to collection of fingerposts at gate.

❹ Go through gate. Cross to enclosed track ('Wolds Way'). Follow this to Huggate Lane into **Fridaythorpe**. Turn **R** along main road then **L** by **Manor House Inn** to the green and **St Mary's Church**.

❺ Return to Huggate Lane; follow lane back to gate by collection of fingerposts. Go through gate and follow **Wolds Way** down dale. Keep to **L** of fence as **Horse Dale** joins from **R**.

❻ Go through gate, ignore Wolds Way going off to **R**, but turn **L** over stile and continue down **Harper Dale**. Pass game breeding area on **L** then bear **R** with rising path to meet track on hill. Bear **R** to cattle grid. Turn **L** and follow track round to **R**. Turn **L** at end and follow track to **Northfield House**.

❼ Walk through yards; follow access road back towards **Huggate**. Continue up lane; turn **L** across green to return to car park.

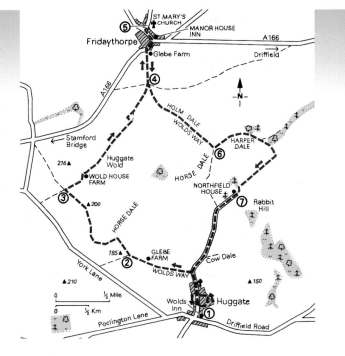

Carl Wark Moorland Ramparts

5½ miles (8.8km) 3hrs Ascent: 328ft (100m)

Paths: Generally good paths
Suggested map: OS Explorer OL1 Dark Peak
Grid reference: SK 252801
Parking: Surprise View car park on A6187 beyond Hathersage

Along medieval packhorse trails in search of the dwelling place of ancient Britons.

① From car park at Surprise View go through kissing gate and uphill on well-worn path. At large group of stones path veers **L** and continues uphill towards **Over Owler Tor**. Just before this, go **L** on smaller track, head downhill towards fence. Turn **R** at fence.

② Continue following track until it meets with dry-stone wall that has been running parallel with track. Follow path **R** towards sheepfold. At end of sheepfold, path veers slightly **R** across moorland. Rocky outcrop of **Higger Tor** is on **L** and Carl Wark in front. The fort is probably of Iron- or Bronze-Age construction and was re-fortified at the end of the Roman occupation.

③ When path intersects another, turn **R**. Continue past Carl Wark, keeping it to **R**. Go downhill towards far **R** corner of wood. Cross stone bridge then wooden bridge, head uphill on well-worn path to join old green road; turn **L**.

④ Continue along road with **Burbage Rocks** above you and to **R**. At **Upper Burbage Bridge** cross 2 streams via large stones, head uphill and follow upper of 2 paths to **L** and uphill. Continue across moorland then ascend **Higger Tor** on stone stepped path. Cross tor then descend other side near southeast corner.

⑤ Follow track across moor towards **Carl Wark**. Ascend and turn **L** to reach summit then return to top of path and, keeping stone ramparts on **L**, continue past cairn and descend via path to southwest.

⑥ From here, path heads across boggy section of moor, curves round small, rocky hill then heads downhill towards **A6187**. Cross on to this via stile, cross road and turn **R** on to pavement. Follow this to next stile on **L**, cross it and continue on path that runs parallel to road.

⑦ When track nears car park go through kissing gate, cross road then continue on grass track back into car park.

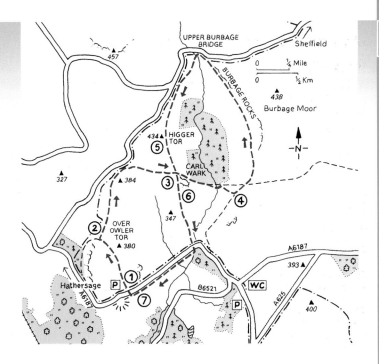

Bradfield Dale Dike Dam Disaster

5½ miles (8.8km) 3hrs 30min Ascent: 394ft (120m)

Paths: Minor roads, bridleways, forest paths
Suggested map: OS Explorer OL1 Dark Peak
Grid reference: SK 262920 **Parking:** By cricket ground in Bradfield

A quiet waterside walk around the site of an horrific industrial tragedy.

① Walk out of car park and then turn **R** on to road. At Y-junction go **R** towards Midhopestones. Walk uphill, following road, passing **Walker House** farm and **Upper Thornseat** passing on R. At entrance to **Thomson House**, when road turns sharply R, turn **L** on to farm road.

② From here go through gate ahead and on to **Hall Lane**, public bridleway. Follow this along edge of wood then through another gate and continue **R** on farm road. Another gate at end of this road leads to entrance to **Hallfield**.

③ Right of way goes through Hallfield's grounds but alternative permissive path leads **L** over stile, round perimeter of house and across another stile to re-join bridleway at rear of house. Follow bridleway crossing stile, gate and then past **Stubbin Farm**.

④ The next gate leads you to **Brogging Farm** and dam at head of **Strines Reservoir**. Look out for sign

near end of farmhouse and turn **L**. Go slightly downhill, over stile, follow path, then cross stile and go through wood.

⑤ Cross stream by footbridge, keep to **R**, ignoring 2nd footbridge. Follow path along bank of **Dale Dike Reservoir** to dam head. Several hundred people were killed and many properties destroyed when the dam collapsed in 1864. It was rebuilt in 1875 but the dam was not brought into full use until 1887 – a very dry year. From here continue through woods, down several sets of steps and continue on path. Look out for **memorial** to those who were killed in the tragedy.

⑥ Follow path until it reaches road. Cross stile, turn **R** on to road; proceed to Y-junction. Turn **R**, cross bridge then look for public footpath sign ('Low Bradfield') just before entrance to **Doe House**. Cross stile on **L** and follow path. Path crosses 2 stiles then terminates at T-junction with **Mill Lee Road** opposite **Plough Inn**. Turn **L** and follow road downhill, through village and back to car park.

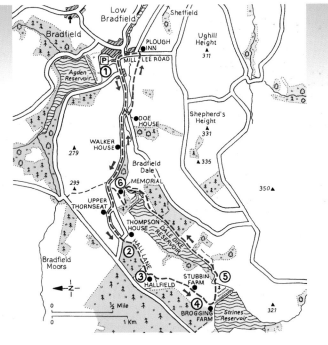

Fairburn Ings Lakes and Birds

5 miles (8km) 2hrs 30min Ascent: 131ft (40m) ⚠

Paths: Good paths and tracks (some newly created from spoil heaps), 7 stiles

Suggested map: OS Explorer 289 Leeds

Grid reference: SE 472278

Parking: Free parking in Cut Road, Fairburn. From A1, drive into village, turn L 100yds (91m) past Three Horseshoes pub

A visit to West Yorkshire's very own 'Lake District', now a bird reserve.

❶ Walk down Cut Road as it narrows to track. Soon you have main lake to R, and smaller stretch of water to L. When track forks, keep R (unless you want to visit 1st of bird hides, in which case detour to L). Path finishes at end of lake, on approaching **River Aire**.

❷ Go R here to join path along top of ridge (old spoil heap), with river to L and lake R. Look out for couple of other bird hides, before you lose sight of lake. Path crosses broader expanse of spoil heap, through scrubland, following river in broad arc to R, before descending to stile above another small mere. Bear R on broad track and drop down into car park of **Fairburn Ings** visitor centre.

❸ Meet road. Go R for 100yds (91m), then go L ('Ledston and Kippax') for just 100yds (91m), and pick up path on R that hugs R-H fringe of wood. Beyond wood, take path between fields; it broadens to track as you approach **Ledsham**. At new housing estate, turn R, along Manor Garth.

❹ You arrive in village by **ancient church**. Walk R, along road (or, for refreshments, go L to **Chequers Inn**). Beyond village, where road bears L, take gate on R, leading to good track uphill. Where main track goes R, into fields, continue along track ahead, into woodland. Leave wood by stile, crossing pasture on grassy track. Cross 2 stiles taking you across narrow spur of woodland.

❺ Head slightly L, uphill, across next field, to follow fence and hedgerow. Continue – soon on better track – across stile. Beyond next stile track bears L, towards farm buildings: but keep straight on, with fence on R, along field path. Go through metal gate then join access track downhill. When you meet road, go L and back into **Fairburn**.

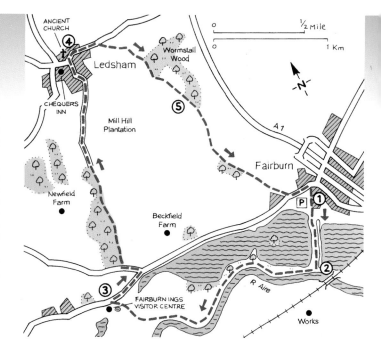

Wetherby The River Wharfe

3½ miles (5.7km) 2hrs Ascent: 65ft (20m) ⚠

Paths: Field paths and good tracks, a little road walking, 1 stile

Suggested map: OS Outdoor Leisure 289 Leeds

Grid reference: SE 405479

Parking: Free car parking in Wilderness car park, close to river, just over bridge as you drive into Wetherby from south

Walk around a handsome country market town with a long history and along a stretch of the mature River Wharfe.

❶ Walk to far end of car park, to follow path with River Wharfe on your R and cliffs to your L. You pass in quick succession beneath shallow arches of 2 modern bridges, carrying **A58** and **A1** roads across **River Wharfe**. Go through kissing gate to continue on riverside path, soon with open fields on L. Take another kissing gate to arrive at Wetherby's **water treatment works**.

❷ Go L here, up track around perimeter fence. After 150yds (138m) you meet metalled track at works' main entrance; go L here. At top of incline, where track bears slightly to R, you have choice of routes. Your path is sharp R, along grassy track between fields. You soon approach wooded slope that overlooks River Wharfe. Take stile, and follow line of trees to farm, Flint Mill Grange. It was here where flints were ground for use in the pottery industry of Leeds. Enter farmyard and take farm access road to L.

❸ Meet **Walton Road** and walk L for 75yds (68m), then go R, along metalled drive (this is signed as a bridleway and the entrance to **Wetherby Racecourse**). After gate you have a choice of routes. Bear L here, downhill, to join the trackbed of the old Church **Fenton-to-Harrogate** railway line, which carried its last train in 1964.

❹ Go L, to enjoy level walking along railway trackbed, until you approach A1 road, raised up on embankment as it skirts around Wetherby. Take underpass beneath road, and bear R along Freemans Way, until you meet Hallfield Lane.

❺ Walk L, along Hallfield Lane, which bears R around **playing fields** of Wetherby **High School** and back into centre of Wetherby and start.

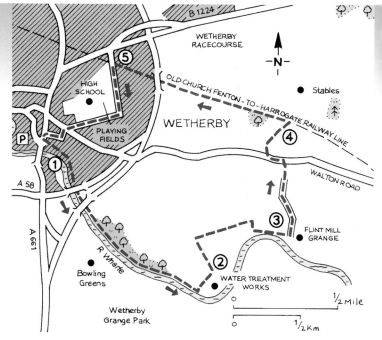

Fulneck Moravian Settlement

4 miles (6.4km) 2hrs Ascent: 262ft (80m) ⚠

Paths: Ancient causeways, hollow ways and field paths, 12 stiles

Suggested map: OS Explorer 288 Bradford & Huddersfield

Grid reference: SE 222306

Parking: Lay-by in Tong village, near church, or on edge of village

A little rural oasis.

❶ From **Tong** village walk up **Keeper Lane** which, beyond gate, becomes sandy track. Walk steadily downhill, following line of old causey stones, into woodland. Cross **Pudsey Beck** on footbridge.

❷ After bridge you have choice of tracks. As you approach waymarker post, continue ahead between stone posts ('**Leeds Country Way**'). Follow beck with **golf course** on **R**. Beyond stile follow field path to another stile, footbridge and meeting of paths. Don't cross bridge, but turn sharp **R** instead, up farm track. Meet road by **Bankhouse Inn**.

❸ Follow road to **R** to see Georgian buildings that make up **Fulneck Moravian settlement**, on ridge with good valley views. 50yds (46m) beyond Fulneck Restaurant go **R**, down lane that soon bends to **R**. At bottom of large brick building look out for steps and footpath downhill. Follow delightful sunken path with hedgerows – and golf fairways – to either side. Come

out on to **golf course**, keeping half **L** across fairway, to rejoin path accompanying **Pudsey Beck**.

❹ After 3 stiles reach ruined **mill**; bear **R** to continue on beckside path. You have easy walking, through fields and scrubland, punctuated by stiles. Leave beck via walled path out on to road.

❺ Go **R** here, passing another mill, to T-junction. Cross over road and take waymarked footpath between gateposts into Sykes Wood. Go **R** through gate ('**Leeds Countryside Way**'). Follow path downhill, soon with **Tong Beck**. After walking about ½ mile (800m) through woodland, take footbridge over beck and walk across field, bearing **L** to stile. Follow path along field edge, then through woodland. Keep **L**, when track forks, to stile. Keep following track – ignoring bridges and side-paths – until you reach stile next to gate and broader track.

❻ Go **R**, uphill, on good track. When you meet road go **L** to arrive back in **Tong** village.

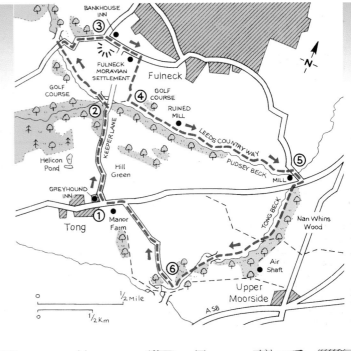

Burley in Wharfedale Giant Footsteps

4 miles (6.4km) 2hrs Ascent: 560ft (170m) ⚠

Paths: Good tracks and moorland paths, 5 stiles

Suggested map: OS Explorer 297 Lower Wharfedale

Grid reference: SE 163457

Parking: Burley in Wharfedale Station car park

The moorland where a giant once lived.

❶ From car park, cross line via footbridge and go **L** along lane. Follow it past houses and between fields up to **Hag Farm**.

❷ When track wheels **R**, into farmyard, keep **L** on track to stile and gate. Accompany wall downhill; after 100yds (91m) take gap stile in wall. Bear off sharply to **R**, to follow stream up to another wall and gap stile. Follow fence uphill to take another stile, cross over stream via footbridge and join approach road to group of houses. Walk uphill to meet **Guiseley–Ilkley road**. Cross road and continue on stony track ahead. After 50yds (46m), ford stream and follow path uphill through woodland, on to path between hedges. Out on to open pasture you come to gate. Follow wall to **R**, soon leaving it to take indistinct path uphill.

❸ Meet stony track; follow it to **R**, along moorland edge. Follow wall to stile by gate. Immediately after, keep **R** when track forks. Keep **R** again as you

approach small brick building. Route finding is now easy, as track wheels around farm. Keep **L** at next farm ('**York View**') to make slow descent, following wall on **R**. As you approach 3rd farm, watch for 2 barns and gate, on **R**. Take indistinct path to **L** here, passing small quarry. Enjoy level walking. Then, go steeply down little ravine and cross beck; continue up other side. Before reaching top, bear **R** and follow path downhill to meet road by sharp bend.

❹ Walk 100yds (91m) down road, to another sharp R-H bend. Bear **L** here ('**Ilkley Moor Garden Centre**'). Keep **L** of garden centre, by continuing down stony track. Keep **L** of house, **R** of **The Lodge**; when track bears sharp **L** towards farm, your route is to **R**, through kissing gate, to follow field path downhill with woodland to **L**. After another kissing gate, follow fence – then wall – on **R**. Beyond 3rd kissing gate and another gate, join tree-lined track heading to **R**.

❺ Meet road and walk downhill back to car park.

Farnley Tyas Castle Hill

4½ miles (7.2km) 2hrs 30min Ascent: 360ft (110m)

Paths: Field paths, a little road walking on quiet lanes, 18 stiles
Suggested map: OS Explorer 288 Bradford & Huddersfield
Grid reference: SE 162125
Parking: 200yds (183m) along Butts Road by church in Farnley Tyas. Park in lay-by by recreation field

Huddersfield's most prominent landmark.

❶ Enter **recreation field**; follow wall to **R**. Pass 2 gates, on to track. At road, turn **R**.

❷ 100yds (91m) past **farm** bear **R** on track. When track bends R, towards **Ludhill Farm**, take path on **L**. Take stile next to gate, keeping **L** across field, to stile, and descend towards houses. Keep **L** at fork of paths; walk between hedgerows, soon bear **L** to path to road.

❸ Go **R**, downhill. Bear **R** after cottages on track into woodland. Bear **L**, after 50yds (46m), on path that descends to stile. Continue across field (aim towards farm); cross stream, then go through woodland. Cross another field (**L** of **High Royd Farm**). Go through gate and join track that leads to road by **High Royd Cottage**. Walk **R** for 100yds (91m). Where road bears **R** take gap stile on **L** by gate; follow path. Take stile by gate; bear **R**, uphill, along field edge; go through gap in wall; cross over another field. Follow edge of next field (hedge left). Path levels out until meets road.

❹ Go **R** for 20yds (18m), then **L** through gap stile. Keeping hedge **R**, follow field-edge path. 150yds (138m) before wood, take waymarked gap in wall **L**. Follow it downhill, over stile; keep to **R-H** edge of next field. Keep ahead at next stile. Go through farmyard; join access track to meet road. Go **R**, downhill. After passing 2 cottages, go through gap stile **R**.

❺ Descend into valley. Take stile and steps; cross **Lumb Dike** via plank bridge. Bear **L** uphill, then **L** to follow river and through **Molly Carr Wood**. Descend to where 2 streams meet (jump 2nd beck). Follow watercourse; cross side-beck. Take few steps to **R**, uphill, to shortly join track, via gate to road.

❻ Go **R**, uphill; 75yds (68m) past sharp **L-H** bend, take track to **R** ('Farnley Bank'). Pass house; when track bears R, to **Farnley Bank Farm**, take stile ahead; follow field path uphill. Meet road; walk **R**, uphill and into **Farnley Tyas**. At T-junction bear **R**, then **L** by church on to **Butts Road**.

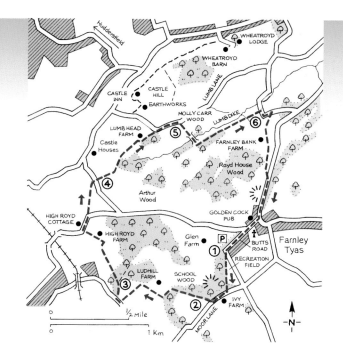

Holmfirth Last of the Summer Wine

4½ miles (7.2km) 2hrs Ascent: 558ft (170m)

Paths: Good paths and tracks, 8 stiles
Suggested map: OS Explorer 288 Bradford & Huddersfield
Grid reference: SE 143084
Parking: Park in Crown Bottom car park (pay-and-display) on Huddersfield Road

Land of Compo, Foggy and Clegg.

❶ From car park, walk to **R** along **Huddersfield Road** for 100yds (91m) then turn **L**, up **Wood Lane**. Road soon narrows to steep track. Keep **L** of house, through gate, to continue on walled path. At top of hill, by bench, follow track to **R** and into valley. Shortly after nearing woodland, there's several tracks: keep **L** on walled path, uphill. Join farm track and, 100yds (91m) before cottage, look for wall stile on **L**. Follow field path to emerge, between houses, in **Upperthong**. Turn **R** into village, past pub to T-junction.

❷ Bear **L** along road, which wheels round to **R**. Walk downhill. After 150yds (138m), take cinder track on **R**. Descend past **Newlands Farm** to road. Cross and take lane ahead, down into valley and up other side. When road forks at top go **R** uphill. Immediately after 1st house, go **L** on sandy track. Follow track to **Lower Hogley Farm**; keep **R**, past houses, to gate and on to field path (wall to L). Cross stile and next field (wall to R). Past next wall stile, veer half **L** across next field (aim for mast). After another field, descend to road.

❸ Go **R** for 50yds (46m) to bear **L** around schoolhouse. Follow walled path downhill, through gate. As path opens out into grassy area, bear **L** on track into valley. Follow high wall on **R**, over stile, on to enclosed path. On approaching houses, take stile and join metalled track at fork. Bear **R**, then immediately **L**, on path between houses. Follow field path through gate, pass houses and mill to meet **A6024**.

❹ Cross road; by cottages take **Old Road** to **L**. Keep ahead at junction down **Water Street**. Beyond **mill**, cross **River Holme** on footbridge; follow riverside path. Soon path veers **R** through pasture; when path forks, keep **R**, uphill, to enter woodland. Continue in same direction, uphill, emerging from wood on to field path. After 2 stiles join track by house. Pass more cottages to meet road.

❺ Go **L** on road to make long descent to **Holmfirth**.

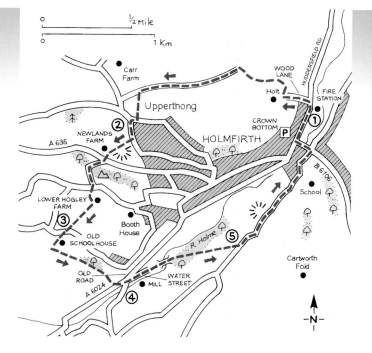

Addingham To a Victorian Spa Town

5½ miles (8.8km) 2hrs 30min **Ascent:** 197ft (60m) ⚠
Paths: Riverside path and field paths, some road walking, 7 stiles
Suggested map: OS Explorer 297 Lower Wharfedale
Grid reference: SE 084498
Parking: Lay-by at eastern end of Addingham, on bend where North Street becomes Bark Lane

Along a stretch of the lovely River Wharfe.

❶ Walk 50yds (46m) then descend steps down to **R** ('**Dales Way**'). Bear **R** again, and cross **River Wharfe**. Follow path along field edge. Cross stream and join track between walls that soon emerges at minor road by sharp bend. Turn **R**; after about ½ mile (800m) of road walking you reach **Nesfield**.

❷ 100yds (91m) beyond last house, and after road crosses stream, bear **L** up track ('**High Austby**'). Immediately take stile between 2 gates. Cross field ahead, keeping parallel to road (ignoring track going **L**, uphill). There is no obvious path; follow wall on **R**, over stile. Beyond conifer plantation, take ladder stile in fence ahead to keep **L** of **Low Austby Farm**.

❸ Cross footbridge; beyond stile you enter woodland. Follow path downhill, leaving wood by step stile. Follow fence uphill, then cross mid-field to stile at far end, to enter woodland. Follow path through trees, before reaching road via wall stile. Descend **R** to

road junction. Go **R** across **Nesfield Road**; take path to **L** of **electricity sub-station**. After few minutes of riverside walking, you reach **Ilkley's** old stone bridge.

❹ Cross bridge; turn **R** on to riverside path ('**Dales Way**'). Proceed, passing **tennis club**. Opposite clubhouse, take footpath to **L**, via kissing gate then pasture. Navigate 7 kissing gates to reach river. Cross footbridge and enter woodland. Cross stream to track. Go **R**, downhill, on track to river. Through kissing gate, follow path (woodland and fence **L**) before joining **A65**.

❺ Follow road by riverside. After almost ½ mile (800m), go **R**, just before terraced houses, on to **Old Lane**. Pass housing, 'Low Mill Village', to find riverside path at far side. Once past **Rectory** on **L**, and **Old Rectory** grounds on **R**, look for kissing gate on **R**. Take steps and follow path to arched bridge over **Town Beck**. Take path across pasture, in front of church, before crossing another bridge, between houses, to re-emerge on **North Street** in **Addingham**.

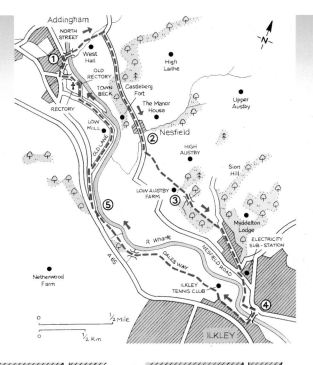

Ilkley Moor Twelve Apostles

4½ miles (7.2km) 2hrs 30min **Ascent:** 425ft (130m) ⚠
Paths: Good moorland paths, some steep paths towards end of walk
Suggested map: OS Explorer 297 Lower Wharfedale
Grid reference: SE 132467
Parking: Off-road parking on Hangingstone Road, opposite Cow and Calf rocks, pay-and-display car park

Discover some ancient standing stones and plenty of history on Ilkley Moor.

❶ Walk along road; 150yds (138m) beyond **Cow and Calf Hotel**, where road bears **L**, fork **R** up grassy path. Scramble up ridge to **Pancake Stone**, and enjoy extensive views back over **Ilkley** and Wharfedale. Bear **R** on path along edge of ridge, cross stony track and pass **Haystack Rock**. From here track slowly wheels **L**, to run parallel to **Backstone Beck**, uphill, on to open heather moorland.

❷ At top, meet **Bradford–Ilkley Dales Way** link path. Go **L** here; soon you are walking on section of duckboarding. Pass boundary stone at top of next rise, and continue to ring of Bronze-Age stones known as **Twelve Apostles**. These stones are the most visible evidence of 7,000 years of occupation of these moors. There are other smaller circles and Ilkley Moor is celebrated for its Bronze-Age rock carvings, many showing the familiar 'cup and rings' designs. The most

famous of the rocks features a sinuous swastika; a symbol of good luck until corrupted by the Nazi movement.

❸ Retrace your steps from **Twelve Apostles**, and continue along **Dales Way** link path. Having crossed **Backstone Beck**, you soon leave open moorland behind, and find yourself on top of ridge. Enjoy views across Ilkley and Wharfedale, before taking path (which is stepped in some places) steeply downhill. Beneath clump of trees you come to **White Wells**.

❹ Bear **R**, passing to **L** of ponds, on path, downhill. Aim for pyramid-shaped rock, after which you emerge on to metalled track. Walk either way around **tarn**. At far end take path, uphill, then down to cross **Backstone Beck** again on little footbridge, then final haul uphill to reach **Cow and Calf rocks**.

❺ It's worth taking a few minutes to investigate the rocks or watch climbers practising their belays and traverses. From here paved path leads to car park.

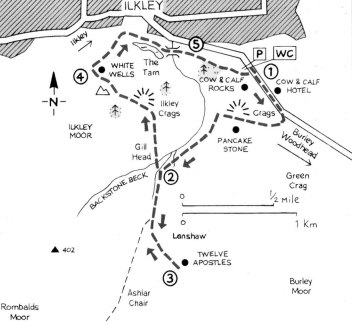

49 Oxenhope Age of Steam

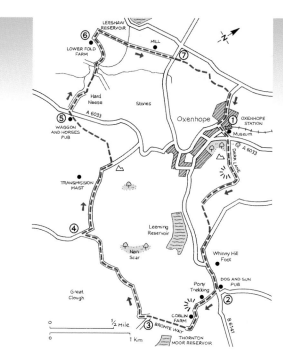

6 miles (9.7km) 3hrs **Ascent:** 492ft (150m)
Paths: Good paths and tracks, 6 stiles
Suggested map: OS Outdoor Leisure 21 South Pennines
Grid reference: SE 033354
Parking: Street parking in Oxenhope, near Keighley and Worth Valley Railway station

Moorland and the Worth Valley Railway.

❶ From **station** entrance take minor road to **L**, to A6033. Cross and take **Dark Lane** ahead, sunken lane that ascends steeply. Follow track to road. Go **R**, downhill, to join Denholme Road (**B6141**). Walk **L** to reach **Dog and Gun** pub then **R** on to Sawood Lane.

❷ At **Coblin Farm**, route becomes rough track. Go through gate to join metalled road to **R**, uphill ('**Brontë Way**'). After 100yds (91m), when road accesses **Thornton Moor Reservoir**, keep ahead on unmade track. Go through gate into rough pasture, ignoring **Brontë Way** sign to R.

❸ At fork, just 50yds (46m) further on, keep **R** as track goes downhill towards **transmission mast** on mid-horizon. Pass clump of trees, and cross watercourse before descending to minor road.

❹ Go **R** here to pass cattle grid and **mast**. 150yds (138m) beyond **mast**, as road begins steep descent, take wall stile on **L**. Go through another wall stile, to

walk **L**, uphill, on broad, walled track to **Waggon and Horses** pub.

❺ Cross road. Take track between gateposts, which bears **R**, steeply downhill. Where it bears sharp **R** again, after 300yds (274m), take stile to **L**, by gate. Follow wall downhill to take 3 stiles; at bottom meet walled path. Go **L** here; cross stream, and continue uphill to arrive at entrance to **Lower Fold Farm**.

❻ Follow farm track to **R**; turn **R** again, 20yds (18m) further on, at end of cottage, to join metalled track. Track soon bears **R** above **Leeshaw Reservoir** and makes gradual descent. Pass mill to meet road.

❼ Cross road and take track ahead ('**Marsh**'). Keep **R** of 1st house, on narrow walled path, then paved path. Pass through courtyard of house as path goes **L**, then **R** and through kissing gate. Follow path between wall and fence to meet walled lane. Go **R** here, passing houses, then on field path to meet road. Go **R** here and back down into **Oxenhope**.

50 Slaithwaite Along the Colne Valley

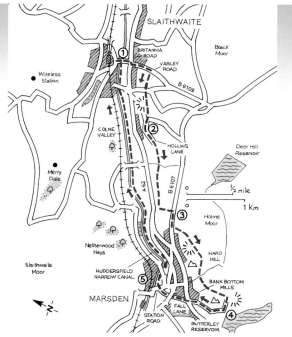

6 miles (9.7km) 2hrs 30min **Ascent:** 550ft (170m)
Paths: Field paths, good tracks and canal tow path, 12 stiles
Suggested map: OS Outdoor Leisure 21 South Pennines
Grid reference: SE 079140
Parking: Plenty of street parking in Slaithwaite

The rural face of the valley.

❶ Walk along **Britannia Road** to A62. Cross, turn **R** and take **Varley Road** to **L**. Beyond last house go **R**, through stile. Join track across field to stile on R-H end of wall. Follow to **R**, cross stile, to minor road. Go **R**; follow road **L** to T-junction. Keep ahead on track then **L** on track between houses. Go through gate on to field path. Follow wall on **R**. Towards its end go through gap in wall; take steps to proceed in same direction. After step stile, keep to **R**, slightly downhill, following wall to stile.

❷ Go **R** at road, then **L** ('**Hollins Lane**'). Track becomes rougher; when it peters out, keep **L** of cottage and through gate. Follow field-edge path ahead, through pair of gates either side of beck. Pass ruined house to descend on walled path. When it bears R keep ahead through gate on to field path. Follow wall on R; where it ends keep ahead, slightly uphill across 2 fields to meet track. Go **L**, towards

farm; then **R**; through stile and pair of gates, on to another walled path. Path soon bears **R**; take stile to **L** to follow field-edge path. Cross another field and go **L**, uphill, at wall. Take stile and follow path to B6107.

❸ Go **R** for just 75yds (68m); take track to **L**. Keep **L** of house, via kissing gate. 150yds (138m) past house, turn **R** at fork, taking less obvious track. Soon follow wall. Across beck, track forks again; keep **L**, uphill, to skirt shoulder of **Hard Hill**. Track descends steeply, then up to stile, then down again to cross beck on stone retaining wall. After another climb, route levels. Bear **L**, steeply uphill, at stone building, cross 2 stiles and meet track. Follow it **R**, downhill, to road.

❹ Go **R**, passing terraced houses. Keep ahead at roundabout, down **Fall Lane**, soon bearing **L**, under main road, into **Marsden**. Take **Station Road**, far end of green, to meet **Huddersfield Narrow Canal**.

❺ Take path on **R**. Follow canal tow path for 3 miles (4.8km) back into **Slaithwaite**.

Rishworth Moor Along Blackstone Edge

5½ miles (8.8km) 2hrs 30min **Ascent: 328ft (100m)** 🄰

Paths: Moorland paths; may be boggy after rain
Suggested map: OS Outdoor Leisure 21 South Pennines
Grid reference: SE 010184
Parking: Small car park above Baitings Reservoir

A bracing ramble on old moorland tracks, with extensive views all the way.

❶ From car park, walk **L** down road. 50yds (46m) after crossing beck, take gate in wall on your **R** ('Booth Wood Reservoir').

❷ Follow tumbledown wall uphill towards **L-H** side of **Blackwood Farm**. Walk between farmhouse and outbuilding, to reach gate at top of farmyard. Walk up next field to stile and then continue steeply uphill, following wall to your **R**. Look for views of **Ryburn Valley**, as you crest hill and arrive at ladder stile, next to gate in wall.

❸ From here you strike off to **R**, across rough moorland; path is distinct but narrow. Keep straight ahead at yellow-topped post (you will see others on route). Walk roughly parallel to M62, heading just to **R** of tall mast on far side of motorway. At next waymarker stick, bear slightly **R**, on less-obvious path. As you start to walk downhill you have good views down to **Green Withens Reservoir** ahead. Descend to cross side-beck on little plank bridge, to meet reservoir drainage channel.

❹ Take bridge over channel and walk **R**, following this watercourse towards reservoir. About 300yds (274m) before reservoir embankment, take bridge back over channel ('Blackstone Edge and Baitings'). Bear slightly **L** to follow path uphill – soon quite steeply – before it levels out and bears **L** around **Flint Hill**. The view behind you recedes; ahead is Upper **Ryburn Valley**. Descend to water channel on your **L** and fork of paths.

❺ Go **R** (sign indicates **Baitings Reservoir**), continuing to skirt hill on good, level path. Keep **L**, where path forks, to begin gradual descent towards **Baitings Reservoir**. When you come to wall corner, keep straight ahead, following wall on your **L**. Soon you are on walled track, passing through 2 gates and finally emerging at little car park above reservoir.

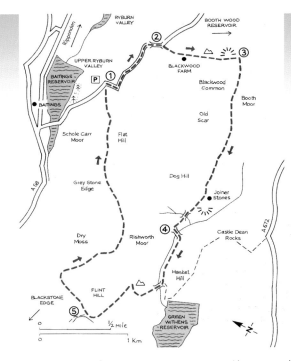

Hardcastle Crags Two Wooded Valleys

5 miles (8km) 2hrs 30min **Ascent: 787ft (240m)** 🄲

Paths: Good paths and tracks, plus open pasture, no stiles
Suggested map: OS Outdoor Leisure 21 South Pennines
Grid reference: SD 988291
Parking: National Trust pay-and-display car parks at Midgehole, near Hebden Bridge (accessible via A6033, Keighley Road)

Walk in a pair of beautiful wooded valleys, linked by a high level path.

❶ Walk along drive, passing **lodge**, and into woods. Take 1st path to **L**, which descends to **Hebden Water**. Follow good riverside path through delectable woodland, passing Hebden Hey – popular picnic site, with stepping stones – to reach **Gibson Mill**. Buildings and mill dam behind are worth investigating.

❷ Join track uphill, to **R** of **Gibson Mill**, soon passing crags that give woods their name. Keep on main track, ignoring side-paths, to leave woodland and meet metalled road. Keep **L** here, still uphill, across beck and approach **Walshaw**, knot of houses, enjoying terrific views.

❸ Just before you reach houses – when you are opposite some barns – bear sharp **R** through gate on to enclosed track ('Crimsworth Dean'). You are soon walking along grassy track crossing pasture, descending to beck and through gate. Walk uphill, soon bearing to **R** as you follow wall around shoulder of **Shackleton Knoll**. Go through gate in wall on your **L**, and continue as path bears **R**, still following wall, but now it's on your **R**. Here you have level walking and great views. Take gate in wall on **R**, just above **Coppy Farm**, to join walled track downhill into valley of **Crimsworth Dean**. You meet more substantial track by another ruin of farm. This track is old road from Hebden Bridge to Haworth: a great walk to contemplate for another day.

❹ Bear **R**, along this elevated track, passing farm on L. Look out, by farm access track to R, for **Abel Cross**: not one but a pair of old waymarker stones. Continue down main track, into **National Trust woodland**, keeping **L**, after field, when track forks. Beyond pair of cottages track is metalled; you soon arrive back at car parks at **Midgehole**.

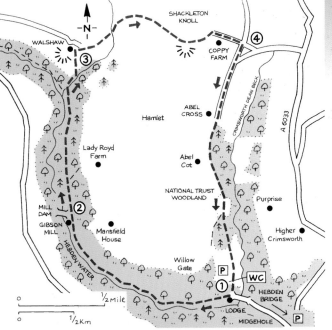

Lydgate The Bridestone Rocks

5 miles (8km) 2hrs 30min Ascent: 984ft (300m)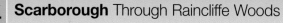
Paths: Moorland and packhorse paths, some quiet roads, 3 stiles
Suggested map: OS Outdoor Leisure 21 South Pennines
Grid reference: SD 924256
Parking: Roadside parking, Lydgate, 1½ miles (2.4km) out of Todmorden, on A646, signposted to Burnley

Ancient tracks and gritstone outcrops.

❶ From **post office**, take **Church Road**. At end go **R**, down drive towards house. Look immediately for path that passes to **R** of house and soon goes beneath arch of railway viaduct. Join stony track, walking steeply uphill, where track is sunken, between walls. Where walls end, track gives on to moorland. Keep **R** on track towards **farm**. Keep **L** of farmhouse, continuing along walled track uphill. At another walled track, go **R** towards outcrop on 1st horizon. Beyond 2 gates you reach open moorland again: **Whirlaw Common**. Cross pasture on section of paved causeway to arrive, via gate, at **Whirlaw Stones**.

❷ Keep to causeway that bears **R**, below stones. Leave **Whirlaw Common** by gate on to walled path. Bear **L** at farm, on track that follows wall uphill. Bear **R** around rocks, to join **Windy Harbour Lane**. Climb steeply, before road levels off to meet **Eastwood Road**. Go **L** here for 150yds (140m). Where wall ends,

take stile on **L**. Grassy path leads to **Bridestones**.

❸ Continue past **Bridestones** passing boulders, before turning **R** to follow indistinct path across rough terrain. At road, you reach **Sportsman's Inn**.

❹ Go **L** along road; you have 1 mile (1.6km) of level walking, passing **Hawks Stones** on **R** and houses, until you reach minor road on **L**. This is **Mount Lane**, ('Shore and Todmorden'). Walk down road and beyond farm on **R**, take good track to **L**, slightly downhill. Look out for **Mount Cross** in field to **L**.

❺ Detour past **Lower Intake Farm** on path, soon enclosed by walls. 200yds (183m) beyond bridge cross stream and look out for stile on **R**, by gate between gateposts. Follow field path downhill, keeping wall to **L**. Grassy track leads under **Orchan Rocks**.

❻ Where wall bears **L**, beyond rocks, follow in downhill to stile. Now join farm track that takes serpentine route downill, through woodland. Your way is clear: down into valley and back into **Lydgate**.

Scarborough Through Raincliffe Woods

5 miles (8km) 2hrs Ascent: 584ft (175m)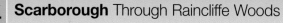
Paths: Field tracks, woodland paths, some steep, 2 stiles
Suggested map: OS Outdoor Leisure 27 North York Moors – Eastern
Grid reference: SE 984875
Parking: Hazelhead picnic site on Mowthorpe Road, near road junction

A woodland walk to a glacial lake.

❶ From picnic site, walk on to road; turn **L**, downhill. After woodland ends, pass houses on **R**, then opposite bungalow, No 5, turn **R** down track to **Thorn Park Farm**. Follow track, as it bends **L** by farm buildings then **R** past cottage to metal gate. Continue following track, which bends **L** then **R**, then through 2 gateways.

❷ Just before next gateway turn **R** and walk up field side to stile beside gateway, which takes you on short path to road. Turn **L**. Follow road to reach next car park on **R**.

❸ Go up through car park towards gate and uphill on path ahead. Where main path bends **R**, go straight ahead, more steeply, to reach crossing, grassy track. Turn **L** through gate and follow path. Where it forks, take **R-H** path.

❹ Look out for path on **L**, which immediately bends **R** over drainage runnel. Path goes down into small

valley. Turn **L**, downhill, then follow path as it bends **R** again, past old quarry. Path descends to reach **Throxenby Mere**. Turn **R** along edge of Mere – part of path is on boardwalks.

❺ Just before you reach picnic place, turn **R** through area bare of undergrowth to take path which goes up steeply until it reaches grassy track at top of hill.

❻ Turn **R** and go through metal gate, then follow path for 1 mile (1.6km), parallel with wall. It passes through gateway with stile by it and eventually reaches gate with public bridleway sign.

❼ Do not go through gate out into fields, but turn **R** and continue in woodland. Where main path swings **L** and another goes **R**, keep ahead, steeply downhill. When path joins another go **L**, down steps and along boardwalk to meet crossing path.

❽ Turn **R**; go down to gate into car park. Turn **L** on to road, and **L** again to junction. Turn **R**, following Harwood Dale sign, for Hazelhead picnic site.

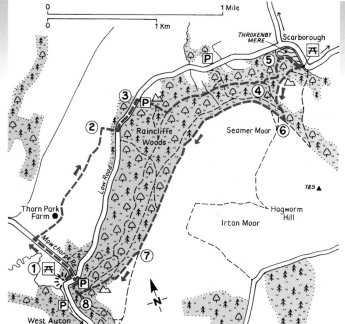

Robin Hood's Bay Along the Coast

5½ miles (8.8km) 2hrs 30min **Ascent:** 466ft (142m) ⚠

Paths: Field and coastal paths, a little road walking, 14 stiles

Suggested map: OS Outdoor Leisure 27 North York Moors – Eastern

Grid reference: NZ 950055

Parking: Car park at top of hill into Robin Hood's Bay, by the old railway station

Along part of the Cleveland Way.

❶ From car park, return via entry road to main road. Turn **L** up hill and, where road bears **L**, take signed footpath to **R** over stile. Walk up fields over 3 stiles to metalled lane.

❷ Turn **R**. Go **L** through signed metal gate. At end of field, path bends **R** to gate in hedge on **L**. Continue down next field, stone wall on **L**. Go **R** at end of field; over stile into green lane.

❸ Cross to another waymarked stile; continue along field edge with wall on **R**. At field end, go over stile on **R** then make for waymarked gate diagonally **L**.

❹ Walk towards farm, through gate; take waymarked track round **R** of buildings to another gate then to waymarked opening beside gate. Continue with stone wall on **R**, through another gate and on to track that eventually bends **L** to waymarked stile.

❺ Continue to another stile, then to footbridge over **beck**. At T-junction by telegraph pole, veer **R**; take

path to **R** of bank. After 50yds (46m), look for signpost ('**Hawsker**') in woodland; follow it **R**. As hedge to **R** curves **L**, go through gap on **R** and over signed stile, walking through field to another stile on to main road.

❻ Go **R** and **R** again, following footpath sign, up metalled lane towards **holiday parks**. Pass **Seaview Caravan Park**, cross old railway track and continue along metalled lane, which bends **R**, goes downhill, crosses stream and ascends to **holiday park**.

❼ Follow footpath sign **R**, then go **L**. Follow metalled track through caravans, eventually leaving track to go **L** to waymarked path. Follow path towards coastline, to reach signpost.

❽ Turn **R** along **Cleveland Way** for 2½ miles (4km). Footpath goes through kissing gate; over 3 stiles; through 2 more kissing gates; past Rocket Post Field to 3 gates by National Trust sign. Go **L** through field gate and past houses to reach main road. Car park is directly opposite.

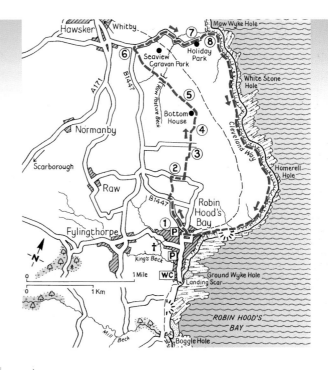

Thixendale A Walk on the Wolds

4 miles (6.4km) 2hrs **Ascent:** 459ft (140m) ⚠

Paths: Clear tracks and field paths, 9 stiles

Suggested map: OS Explorer 300 Howardian Hills & Malton

Grid reference: SE 842611

Parking: Thixendale village street near the church

From the hidden village of Thixendale over chalk hills and through typical dry valleys.

❶ From church, walk west along **Thixendale's** village street. Just beyond last house on **R**, go up track, following sign ('**Wolds Way/Centenary Way**'). Cross over ladder stile in wire fence on your **R** and continue walking up track as it curves round past television aerial.

❷ As you approach top of hill, watch out on **L** for Wolds Way sign, which takes you **L** along grassy track. Go over ladder stile then along field side to meet track again. Continue straight ahead.

❸ At next Wolds Way sign go over stile. Continue with wire fence on **L**. At top of field go **R** by sign. Path descends to reach wooden ladder stile and descends steeply into dry valley to another waymarked stile, then curves to stile by gate.

❹ Follow blue public bridleway sign to **R**, winding **L** up side valley. Near top of valley is deep earthwork

ditch, cross over stile and continue along edge of field. Where footpath divides go **R** through patch of woodland on to track by signpost.

❺ Turn **R** and follow signs ('**Wolds Way**'). Follow clear track for ¾ mile (1.2km). At end of woodland on your **R**, look out for signpost. Turn **R** here, now following **Centenary Way**, going down edge of field and passing ruined building with tall chimney. Follow winding footpath past signpost.

❻ At next signpost turn **R** off track ('**Centenary Way**'). Walk down field side on grassy track. At field end leave track and go through waymarked gate. Path goes **L** and passes along hillside to descend to stile beside gate.

❼ Follow yellow waymark straight ahead across field, to pass over track up hillside **L** of row of trees. Path descends to village cricket field on valley floor. Go over stile by gate, on to lane by house. When you reach main road, turn **R** back to start.

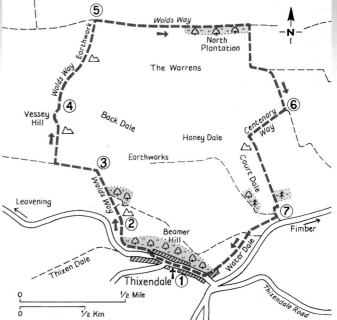

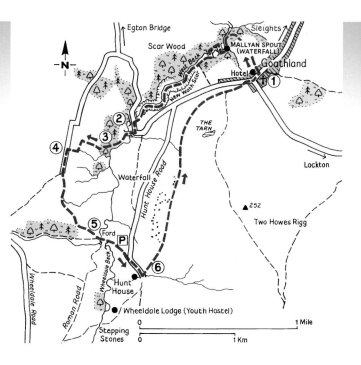

Goathland Mallyan Spout and Moorland

4½ miles (7.2km) 2hrs Ascent: 557ft (167m)

Paths: Streamside tracks, field and moorland paths, 2 stiles

Suggested map: OS Outdoor Leisure 27 North York Moors – Eastern

Grid reference: NZ 827007

Parking: West end of Goathland village, near church

From the moorland village of Goathland, used as the setting for the popular television series *Heartbeat*, through woodland and over the moor.

❶ From opposite church go through kissing gate beside **Mallyan Spout Hotel** ('Mallyan Spout'). Follow path to streamside signpost and then turn **L**. Continue past **waterfall** (take care after heavy rain). Follow footpath signs and cross over 2 footbridges then over stile and up steps, to ascend to stile on to road beside bridge.

❷ Turn **L** along road and climb hill. Where road bends **L**, go **R** along bridleway through gate. Turn **L** down path to go over bridge, then ahead between buildings, through gate and across field.

❸ Part-way across field, go through gate to **R** into woodland. Ascend stony track; go through wooden gate to reach facing gate as you leave wood. Do not go through gate, but turn **R** up field, going **L** at top

through gateway. Continue with wall on your **R** and go through waymarked gateway in wall and up field, to emerge through gate on to metalled lane.

❹ Turn **L** along lane, go through gate and follow sign ('**Roman Road**'). Go through another gate, still following public bridleway signs as you join green lane. Continue through small handgate, to descend to another gate and then on until you reach **ford**.

❺ Cross ford and go straight ahead along track, eventually to reach farm buildings. Turn **R** up road and, just before wooden garage, turn **L** on green track up hillside.

❻ Go straight ahead at crossing track, passing small cairn and bending **L** along ridge. Path is obvious and is marked by series of little cairns. Eventually take **L** fork where path divides, to go down small gill and join clear track. **Goathland church** soon comes into sight. Pass bridleway sign and descend to road near church to return to start.

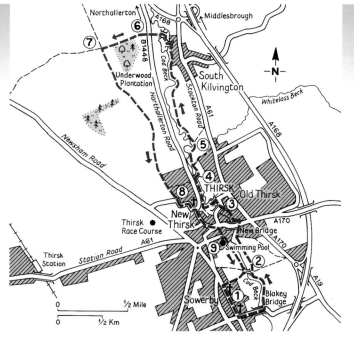

Thirsk Herriot's Darrowby

5 miles (8km) 2hrs Ascent: 66ft (20m)

Paths: Town paths, field paths and tracks, 6 stiles

Suggested map: OS Explorer 302 Northallerton & Thirsk

Grid reference: SE 430813

Parking: Roadside parking in the main street of Sowerby village

James Herriot based his fictional home town on his real one – Thirsk.

❶ Walk down street, away from **Thirsk**. Just past Methodist Church on **L**, go **L** down Blakey Lane. After **bridge** turn **L** through kissing gate. Go through 4 kissing gates to reach footbridge.

❷ Continue along path, with stream on **L**, to stile. Go through 2 gates to car park, keeping ahead to road. Cross it and take path that curves **L** then **R** by bridge. At paved area turn **R**, to go alongside green to road.

❸ Cross and continue beside houses, going **L** at top of green. Cross metal bridge and continue beside **beck** opposite east end of church. Before reaching road take path to **R**, beside bench, to footbridge on **R**.

❹ Cross bridge, go through 2 gates and curve **L** to follow **beck** to gate by bridge. Go ahead (not over bridge). Go over fields, veering slightly **R** to stile on **R**.

❺ Go over stile; follow stream, crossing another 2 stiles to pass beside houses. Continue **L** over

footbridge by mill buildings. Path winds **R** to 2nd footbridge. Follow bridleway sign across field through 2 more gates to reach main road.

❻ Cross road; go through signed gate opposite, to another gate beside wood. At open space, past wood, turn **L** through gap in hedge, opposite waymark to **R**.

❼ Walk down field with hedge on **L**. In 2nd field, go **L** over stile. Continue with hedge on **R** to another stile. Bear **L** to meet path that crosses field and becomes grassy lane between hedges, then track.

❽ At metalled road keep ahead, bearing **L** then **R** past church tower. Turn **R**; walk into town centre. In Market Place head half **L** towards Three Tuns Inn then down signed passageway by drycleaners.

❾ Cross road diagonally **R**; go towards **swimming pool** entrance. Turn **L**; bend round pool building to gate. Proceed to gate and alongside **beck**. At bridge turn **R** across field on grassy track to gate on to lane. Keep ahead to return to **Sowerby**.

North Yorkshire • Northern England

Greenhowe The Mines

6 miles (9.7km) 2hrs 45min Ascent: 1,181ft (360m)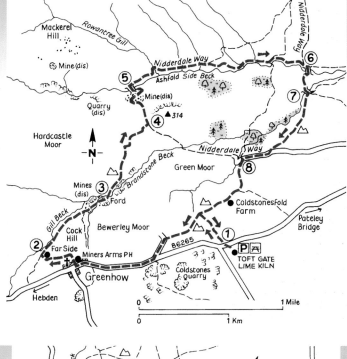

Paths: Field and moorland paths and tracks, 5 stiles

Suggested map: OS Explorer 298 Nidderdale

Grid reference: SE 128643

Parking: Car park at Toft Gate Lime Kiln

Through an industrial landscape.

❶ Cross road from car park; go over stile opposite into field. Follow faint path downhill, over gate in wall and to **R** of barn. Cross another stile; descend to track. Turn **L**; walk up hill through 2 gates to road. Turn **L**; walk up to main road. Turn **R**; follow this past burial ground and **Miners Arms** pub. About 100yds (91m) after pub, just past converted chapel, take lane to **R**. At junction go **L**; follow lane to cattle grid and through gate. Curve **R**, round behind farmhouse.

❷ Follow track downhill into valley of **Gill Beck** and then **Brandstone Beck**. Where track swings **L**, go ahead down valley to reach main track near concrete building. Go **R** of building. Just beyond, proceed down valley to **ford**.

❸ Cross, then follow obvious track up hill. Cross stile beside gate by trees then, 100yds (91m) beyond, take another stile on **R**. Follow track towards farm, going **L** between stone walls. Descend to stile on to track.

❹ Turn **L**, through waymarked gateway. By spoil heap follow track to **R** and downhill. Veer slightly **L**, past iron cogwheel, to cross **Ashfold Side Beck** on concrete causeway to gate.

❺ Follow bridleway sign **R**. Climb hill, to **Nidderdale Way** sign. Turn **R** along track to gate. Wind round valley head, via 2 gateways and 3 cattle grids. Just beyond 3rd, go through gate to **R**. Cross bridge.

❻ Go ahead; bear **L** to gate; follow track uphill and **L** to wall. Turn **R** at end of wall along lane between walls. Continue on track to gate; cross footbridge.

❼ Turn **R** through gate; follow track uphill, passing through another gate. Turn **L** at track, making towards farmhouse, but bear **R** across grass to meet metalled lane. Turn **R**; follow lane over cattle grid.

❽ About 100yds (91m) beyond farm on **R**, turn **L** up path. After cattle grid go **R**; follow track through gate. At **Coldstonesfold Farm** turn **R**; follow track uphill through gate. Go **L** over stile to retrace outward route.

Reeth Heart of Swaledale

5½ miles (8.8km) 2hrs Ascent: 508ft (155m)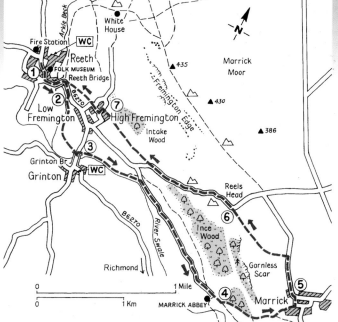

Paths: Field and riverside paths, lanes and woodland, 14 stiles

Suggested map: OS Outdoor Leisure 30 Yorkshire Dales – Northern & Central

Grid reference: SE 039993

Parking: In Reeth, behind fire station, or by the Green

Farmers, miners, knitters and nuns all played important roles in the history of this part of Swaledale.

❶ Spend some time exploring **Reeth** and perhaps visit the **Folk Museum**. For a long time, sheep were the basis of **Reeth's** prosperity and their wool was used in its knitting industry. It also had a vital lead mining industry. From Green, walk downhill, in direction of Leyburn, to **Reeth Bridge**. Over bridge, continue along road as it swings **R**. After 100yds (91m), turn **R** at footpath sign to **Grinton Bridge**.

❷ Follow path through gate and across fields to ascend steps and through gate on to bridge. Turn **L**, cross road and take track beside bridge.

❸ Follow riverside path over 4 stiles, on to metalled lane. Turn **R** and follow lane to **Marrick Abbey**. Walk past buildings, over cattle grid, and turn **L** through gate ('**Marrick**'). In the Middle Ages, it was one of the most important churches in the Dales and home to a group of Benedictine nuns.

❹ Walk up grassy track, through wooden gate and up paved path through woodland. Go through gate, up path and through 3 more gates. Opposite Harlands House turn **L** up metalled road, and **L** again at T-junction.

❺ Follow road for ¼ mile (400m), and turn **L** over stile at footpath sign. Walk up field, going **R** over waymarked, gated stile and follow wall, to go over another gated stile. Continue over further stile by metal gate, then through 2nd metal gate on to road.

❻ Turn **L** and follow road for ¾ mile (1.2km). Where road bends **L**, turn **R** through stile ('**Fremington**'). Follow path through fields, going through gate, to another stile, then along path to lane.

❼ Turn **L**. At houses turn **R**, and as lane bends **L**, go ahead to stile by gate. Keep by wall on **L**, and follow path through 4 stiles back to **Reeth Bridge**. Cross bridge and follow road back to Green.

61 West Burton Villages, Falls and Follies

4 miles (6.4km) 1hr 30min Ascent: 394ft (120m) 🔺

Paths: Field and riverside paths and tracks, 35 stiles

Suggested map: OS Outdoor Leisure 30 Yorkshire Dales – Northern & Central

Grid reference: SE 017867

Parking: Centre of West Burton, by (but not on) the Green

A diverse walk to the famous Aysgarth Falls.

❶ Leave Green near shop. Opposite ('Meadowcroft') go **L** ('Eshington Bridge'). Cross road, turn **R** then **L**, through gate and down steps. Pass barn, through gateway and across field. Go through gap in wall with stile beyond then bend **R** to stile on to road.

❷ Turn **L**, go over bridge and ahead up narrow lane. As it bends **L** go ahead through stile ('**Aysgarth**') then on through gated stile. Proceed to gap in fence near barn, then through gate. Bend **L** to gate in field corner then go through gateway and on to stile. Turn **R**; descend to signpost.

❸ Proceed to stile in field corner. Follow signpost uphill to gateway; go through stile on **R**. Cross field half **L** to go through gated stile to lane. Turn **L**, then almost immediately **R** through stile ('**Aysgarth**'). Go through 3 stiles to road.

❹ Turn **R** into village, past **George and Dragon**. At **L** bend, go ahead toward **chapel**, then **R** at green; follow lane. Go through stile by Field House to another stile, turning **L** along track. Follow path through 8 stiles to road.

❺ Go ahead into churchyard, pass **R** of **church**; go through 2 stiles, through woodland, then over stile. Follow path downhill towards river, descending steps to gate, then stile. When footpath reaches river bank, take signed stile **R**.

❻ Follow path over 2 stiles to signpost, bending **R** across road to road. Turn **L** over bridge, turning **R** into woodland few paces beyond ('**Edgley**'). Cross stile and field to gate to road.

❼ Turn **R**. About 150yds (137m) along, go **L** over stile ('**Flanders Hall**'). Walk below follies on ridge to footpath sign, cross track; go uphill to stile with steps.

❽ Opposite stone barn go **R**, through gate; go downhill through 2 gates, then over 3 stiles to lane. Turn **R**. Go over bridge to join village road. Turn **L**, back to Green.

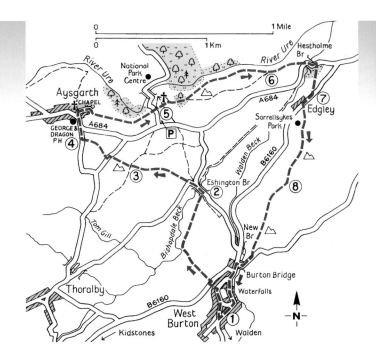

62 Hubberholme Dalesfolk Traditions

5 miles (8km) 2hrs Ascent: 394ft (120m) 🔺

Paths: Field paths and tracks, steep after Yockenthwaite, 11 stiles

Suggested map: OS Outdoor Leisure 30 Yorkshire Dales – Northern & Central

Grid reference: SD 927782

Parking: Beside river in village, opposite church (not church parking)

From JB Priestley's favourite Dales village, along Langstrothdale.

❶ Literary pilgrims should visit the George Inn in **Hubberholme**, where JB Priestley enjoyed the local ale, and the churchyard, the resting place for his ashes. To start, go through Dales Way signed gate near east end of church, bend **L** and then take lower path ('**Yockenthwaite**'). Walk beside river for 1¼ miles (2km) through 3 stiles, gate and 2 more stiles. Path eventually rises to another stone stile into **Yockenthwaite**.

❷ Go through stile and bend **L** to wooden gate. Continue through farm gate by sign to Deepdale and Beckermonds. Before track reaches bridge go **R** and swing round to sign to **Cray** and **Hubberholme**.

❸ Go up hill and, as track curves **R**, continue to follow **Cray** and **Hubberholme** sign. Partway up hill go **R** at footpath sign through wooden gate in fence.

❹ Go through 2nd gate to footpath sign and ascend hillside. Go through gap in wall by another signpost and follow obvious path through several gaps in crossing walls. Go over 2 stone stiles and ascend again to footbridge between stiles.

❺ Cross bridge and continue through woodland to another stile. Wind round head of valley and follow signpost to **Cray**. Go over footbridge. Footpath winds its way down valley side. Go through gate and straight ahead across meadowland to gateway on to track, and on to stone barn.

❻ Bend to **R** beyond barn, down to public footpath sign to **Stubbing Bridge**. Go down path between stone walls and through wooden gate and on to grassy hillside. Pass another footpath sign and continue downhill to meet stream by **waterfall**.

❼ Continue along streamside path through woodland. Go over wooden stile and on past barn to stone stile on to road. Turn **R** along road back to parking place in **Hubberholme**.

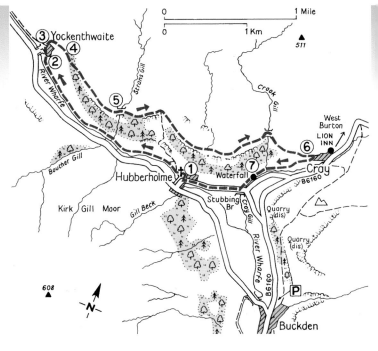

Semerwater Legendary Glacial Lake

5 miles (8km) 2hrs **Ascent:** 853ft (260m)

Paths: Field paths and tracks, steep ascent from Marsett, 19 stiles

Suggested map: OS Outdoor Leisure 30 Yorkshire Dales – Northern & Central

Grid reference: SD 921875

Parking: Car park at the north end of the lake

Legends boast that an angel, disguised as a beggar, drowned the town when he was refused food – the only survivors were a poor couple, who had shown him kindness.

❶ Turn **R** out of car park up road. Opposite farm buildings go **R** over ladder stile ('Stalling Busk'). Go through gated stile and ahead towards barn, then through 2 stone stiles. Just beyond 2nd stile is Wildlife Trust sign. Continue over 2 more stiles to gate.

❷ Just beyond gate, follow **Marsett** sign to corner of field and over gated stone stile. Follow waymarked path as it curves beside river, to barn. Go over stile above barn to stile. Go across field to another stile. Proceed towards barn then go across stream bed.

❸ Immediately afterwards, turn **R** down well-worn footpath, which curves towards roofless barn. Cross 3 stiles, then turn **R**, following path to trees, with stone wall on R. Continue over 2 stiles to footbridge; go straight on to track, then turn **R** to reach **ford**.

❹ Before ford, veer **L** over footbridge and back on to track, which winds into **Marsett**. Just before village, follow stream as it goes **R**, and make for road by red telephone box. Turn **R** over bridge. 100yds (91m) beyond take track ('Burtersett and Hawes') and not path by river.

❺ Walk uphill to gate on **R** at start of stone wall. Go over stile, then continue uphill, over 3 stiles. Soon after steep path flattens out, you reach track that crosses path, coming through gap in wall on **L**.

❻ Turn **R** along track and then go through gate in wall. Where it divides, take **R** fork downhill to stile. Path descends steeply through 2 gates, to reach crossing track. Continue straight ahead. Follow track as it bends **L** to gate on to metalled road.

❼ Turn **R** and then follow road downhill to staggered crossroads, turning **R**, then **L** ('**Stalling Beck**'). Go down hill, cross over bridge and then continue back to car park.

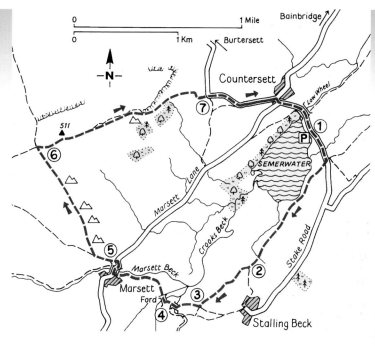

Keld A Riverside Circuit High in the Dales

6 miles (9.7km) 2hrs 30min **Ascent:** 820ft (250m)

Paths: Field and riverside paths and tracks, 10 stiles

Suggested map: OS Outdoor Leisure 30 Yorkshire Dales – Northern & Central

Grid reference: NY 892012

Parking: Signed car park at west end of village near Park Lodge

A classic walk in Upper Swaledale from Keld to Muker along Kidsdon Side, and back by the river.

❶ Walk back down car park entrance road, and straight ahead down gravel track ('**Muker**'). Around **Muker**, you will see traditional hay meadows. They are an important part of the farmer's regime and help maintain the wide variety of wild flowers that grow in them, which is why signs ask you to keep to single file as you walk through them. Continue along at upper level, ignoring path downhill to **L**. Go through gate, pass sign to **Kisdon Force**, and continue along track to signpost.

❷ Turn **R**, following **Pennine Way** National Trail. Path goes through gated stone stile, then through gap in wall to continue with wall on your **L**. Go on through gate and over 4 stiles to descend towards **Muker** to reach signpost where **Pennine Way** goes **R**.

❸ Go straight on down track ('**Muker**'), between stone walls. Go through wooden gate, still following bridleway to **Muker**. Track becomes metalled, as it descends through 2 gates and into walled lane in village to T-junction.

❹ Turn **L** and **L** again by sign to **Gunnerside** and **Keld**. Follow paved path through 5 stiles to reach river. Turn **R** and go over stile to footbridge.

❺ Walk up steps beyond footbridge and turn **L** ('**Keld**'). Follow course of river along clear track, until it curves **R** around **Swinner Gill**, over footbridge by remains of lead workings, and through wooden gate.

❻ Go straight ahead up hill and into woodland. Track eventually winds **L** then **R** round stone barn, then downhill through wooden gate to reach another gate above **Kisdon Force**.

❼ Go **L** by wooden seat, at sign to **Keld**. Follow stream down to footbridge. Go through gate and turn **R**, walk uphill to T-junction, where you turn **R** and proceed to follow path back to car park.

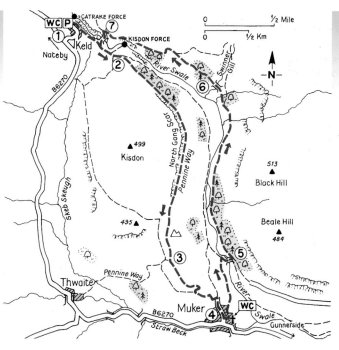

65 Stainforth Forces of Nature

4¾ miles (7.7km) 2hrs Ascent: 525ft (160m)

Paths: Green lanes, field and riverside paths, some road, 15 stiles

Suggested map: OS Explorer OL2 Yorkshire Dales – Southern & Western

Grid reference: SD 821672

Parking: Pay-and-display car park in Stainforth, just off B6479

From an attractive, stone-built village in the heart of the Ribble Valley, with a visit to two impressive waterfalls.

❶ From car park turn **R**, then **R** again ('Settle'). Cross over bridge, go **L** through gap in wall. Follow beck to open area. Go through white posts and turn **L**. Go **R** of green then turn **R**. Go uphill on lane for ¾ mile (1.2km) to gate and ladder stile. (To visit Catrigg Force, take smaller gate to **L**. Return to same point.)

❷ Go over ladder stile. Track bends **R**. Go over stile to cross wall; turn **R** ('Winskill'). Path bears **L** to join track. Go over stile and continue to **farmhouses** then keep ahead over stile ('**Stainforth and Langcliffe**'). As track bends R, go **L** over stile ('**Langcliffe**').

❸ Cross field to stone stile, turning **R** immediately afterwards, to follow path downhill. After short walled section, path descends more steeply to handgate then bears **L** halfway down hill, to descend to handgate. Follow path beyond to another gate.

❹ After gate, lane becomes walled. At crossroads of paths near village, keep ahead. At **Langcliffe's** main street turn **R** and walk to main road.

❺ Cross road and go through gap in wall diagonally **R**. Follow footpath over railway footbridge. Where path ends go towards **mill**. Just before buildings take signed path **R**, behind mill and beside millpond. Go through gate and continue along pond side and through gate to reach gate on **L** by houses.

❻ Go through gate and turn **R** between rows of cottages. Where row ends, before post box, go **L** over footbridge over **River Ribble** and at end turn **R**, beside **weir**, to stone stile ('**Stainforth**'). Follow riverside path, going over 6 more stiles to **caravan site**.

❼ Go **R** of site, on riverside path, past Stainforth Force to humpback Stainforth Bridge. Go through stile on to lane, turn **R** over bridge and follow narrow lane as it bends and climbs to main road. Turn **R** and take 2nd turning **L** back to car park.

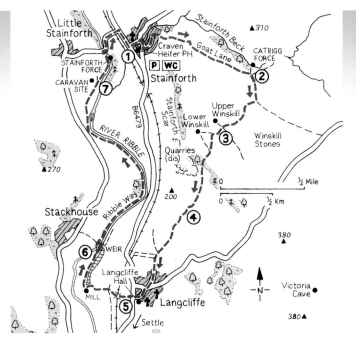

66 Austwick Erratic Progress

5½ miles (8.8km) 2hrs 30min Ascent: 558ft (170m)

Paths: Field and moorland paths, tracks, lanes on return, 10 stiles

Suggested map: OS Outdoor Leisure 2 Yorkshire Dales – Southern & Central

Grid reference: SD 767684

Parking: Roadside parking in Austwick village

Along ancient tracks to the Norber Erratics.

❶ From green in centre of **Austwick**, walk northwards out of village ('Horton in Ribblesdale'). Pass Gamecock Inn and, just past cottage, 'Hob's Gate', turn **L** up Town Head Lane. Just after road bends round to R, go **L** over waymarked ladder stile.

❷ Walk through field to another stile and on to another stile on to lane. Turn **R**. Just before reaching metalled road turn **L** over ladder stile. Follow line of track. As track veers L, go straight on, following line of stone wall to stone stile by gate.

❸ Go through gate; continue along rocky track. Where stone wall on L bends L, by very large boulder across path, go **R** on track to pass R-H edge of **scar**. At signpost, go **L** ('Norber').

❹ Follow path uphill, to plateau; explore **Norber Erratics**. Return same way, back to signpost. Turn **L** ('Crummack'). Follow track as it winds downhill then up beside wall by scar to stone stile on **R**.

❺ Descend to another stile; follow path beneath rocky outcrop, which goes downhill with wall to **L** to reach ladder stile on to metalled lane. Cross lane; go over another ladder stile opposite.

❻ Turn **L** across field. Go over 2 ladder stiles then cross farm track and ridge of rock to stone stile then ladder stile. Cross stile and on to track. Turn **R**. Cross ford on clapper bridge.

❼ Follow track between walls for ½ mile (800m) into **Wharfe**. Turn **L** by bridleway sign in village; follow road round to **R** and down village approach road to reach metalled road. Turn **R**. After 100yds (91m) turn **L** at bridleway sign to **Wood Lane**, down road to **Wood End Farm**.

❽ By farm buildings track goes **R**. Follow it, as it bends **L** and **R** to crossroads of tracks. Go straight ahead, following line of telegraph poles. Track winds to reach metalled lane into village. Turn **R** over bridge to village centre.

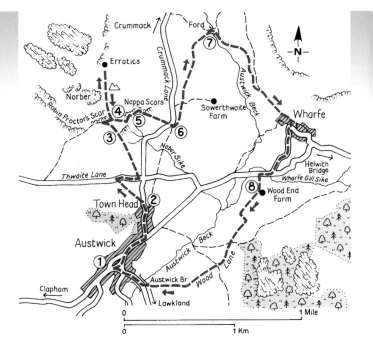

Ribblehead A Majestic Viaduct

5 miles (8km) 2hrs Ascent: 328ft (100m)
Paths: Moorland and farm paths and tracks, 2 stiles
Suggested map: OS Outdoor Leisure 2 Yorkshire Dales – Western
Grid reference: SD 765792
Parking: Parking space at junction of B6255 and B6479 near Ribblehead viaduct

Beside and beneath a great monument to Victorian engineering, opened in 1876 by the Midland Railway.

❶ From parking place, cross road and take boardwalk by sign towards **viaduct** to track. Turn R and follow track until it turns under **viaduct**; continue straight ahead.

❷ Continue walking, now parallel with railway line above you to your L. Go past Three Peaks signboard, following **Whernside** sign. Go over gated wooden stile and continue until you reach railway signal. Go L under railway arch, following public bridleway sign.

❸ Go through gate at end of arch and follow track downhill towards stream, then bear L towards farm buildings. Go through gate between buildings and on to humpback bridge by cottage.

❹ Follow lane over 2 cattle grids. Go through wooden gate by barn then through metal gate, to wind through farm buildings. Go through another metal gate and waymarked wooden gate.

❺ Walk along track through fields, going over small bridge of railway sleepers. By sign to Scar End, bear R to small gate. Go across 3 fields, through series of gates and continue ahead through next field, to reach farm buildings.

❻ Turn L by farm down farm track. Where it bends R, go over cattle grid and turn sharp L round fence and on to track, following bridleway sign to reach ladder stile.

❼ Track is obvious as it winds through fields to reach stream bed (dry in summer). Cross this, and continue along track to meet road near cattle grid. Turn L and walk down road and over bridge.

❽ Where road divides, go R, through gate, towards **viaduct**. At next gate go R again over footbridge by **farm** buildings. Continue through 2 more gates and follow track under viaduct. Continue towards road and parking place.

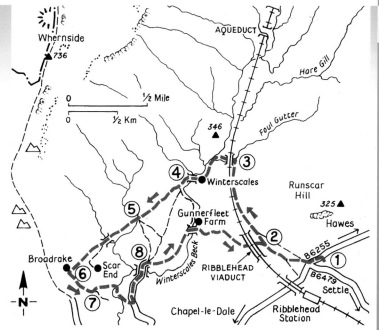

Ingleton The Falls

5 miles (8km) 2hrs Ascent: 689ft (210m)
Paths: Good paths and tracks, with some steps throughout
Suggested map: OS Explorer OL2 Yorkshire Dales – Southern & Western
Grid reference: SD 693733
Parking: Pay-and-display car park in centre of Ingleton, or at start of Waterfalls Walk Ingleton. Admission charge for Waterfalls Walk

By the falls, on a route opened in 1885.

❶ Leave car park in centre of **Ingleton** at its western end. Turn R along road and follow signs ('Waterfalls Walk'), which take you downhill and across river to entrance to falls. Walk through car park, pay admission fee and go through 2 kissing gates. Path goes downwards then ascends steps. Cross **Manor Bridge** and continue upstream, now with river on your L, to **Pecca Bridge**.

❷ Cross bridge, and turn R, back on to L bank of stream. Continue to follow path as it climbs uphill to reach **Thornton Force**. Path winds slightly away from stream and up steps to pass waterfall, and then takes you over **Ravenray Bridge**, and up more steps, to kissing gate and on to **Twisleton Lane**.

❸ Turn R along rough lane. Go through 2 gates, after which track becomes metalled. Walk past farm buildings, following signs for 'Waterfalls Walk'. Go over gated stone stile and along track, then through kissing gate and on to road.

❹ Go across road ('Skirwith'). Follow path as it bends R, still following 'Waterfall Walk' sign. Go through gate, then another into woodland. Path passes **Beezley Falls** and Rival Falls. Little further down, take path to L on to footbridge with good view of deep and narrow Baxenghyll Gorge. Continue to follow path, which takes you to another footbridge.

❺ Cross bridge, go through kissing gate. Follow path as it bends, at one point almost at water level, then going away from water into trees. Path eventually leads through former **quarry** workings. Continue through handgate on to lane.

❻ Beyond gate follow lane that soon enters Ingleton.

❼ Bear R, through houses and back into village, bearing L under railway viaduct and back to car park.

69 Bordley The Monks' Road

5 miles (8km) 2hrs Ascent: 436ft (133m) ⚠

Paths: Tracks and field paths. 2 stiles

Suggested map: OS Explorer OL2 Yorkshire Dales – Southern & Western

Grid reference: SD 951652

Parking: Roadside parking, before gate across lane from Skirethorns

A walk around remote farmsteads and on an old walled green lane, with monastic origins, between Malhamdale and Wharfedale.

❶ From parking place go through gate; follow metalled lane downhill to crossroad of tracks. Turn **R** here ('Kilnsey'). Follow track parallel with dry-stone wall on R to reach crossing track at another signpost at **Mastiles Gate**.

❷ Turn **L** along lane ('**Mastiles Lane**'). At next signpost continue ahead through gate and on to another gate. In 100yds (91m) beyond gate turn **L** through gate in wall and follow track with fence on L. Track eventually goes between walls to gate.

❸ Go through gate. Follow track, which bears **R** by large triangular **boulder**. After 200yds (183m), pass through gateway; turn **L** going to **L** of bungalow down to large **standing stone** near **Middle Laithe**. Turn **L** through farmyard; go over cattle grid. Follow farm track, crossing 2nd cattle grid by National Trust sign

for **New House** farm.

❹ Continue along walled lane into farmyard of **New House**. Go through gate then bear half **R** to go down field to gate in bottom **L-H** corner. Go through gate, turn **L**. Follow line of telegraph poles. Go over stile; descend across stream.

❺ Follow path on other side of stream, to **R** to telegraph poles. Path eventually follows wall on your R. Go through 1st gate on **R**; follow wall on L, bearing **R** to go through gap in crossing wall.

❻ Bear **L** to go round angle of wall on L to stone stile in crossing wall. Follow wall on L up field, past tumbled wall, to join track.

❼ Turn **R** along track, going through 2 gates. After 2nd gate bend **R**; then go **L** at blue waymark sign and through **farm** buildings through double gates. Beyond gates turn **R**; follow track past farmhouse. Climb track, going through gate, then descend to another gate. Turn **R** to crossroads and ascend hill back to start.

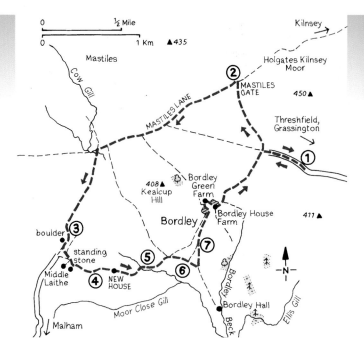

70 Bolton Abbey River and Woodland

6¾ miles (10.9km) 2hrs 30min Ascent: 870ft (265m) ⚠

Paths: Field and moorland paths, then riverside paths, 4 stiles

Suggested map: OS Explorer OL2 Yorkshire Dales – Southern & Western

Grid reference: SE 071539

Parking: Main pay-and-display car park at Bolton Abbey

Over moorland and alongside the Strid to the romantic priory.

❶ Leave car park at its north end and go past **Village Store** and telephone box. Turn **R**, walk down **L** side of green; turn **L**. Pass under archway. Opposite battlemented **Bolton Hall**, turn **L** on to track through signed gate. At top of track, go through gate on **R** with bridleway sign. Walk half **L** to pass corner of some **pools**. Continue through gate beyond; turn **R** towards another gate into wood.

❷ Go through gate and follow signed track through wood to another gate out into field. Follow blue waymarks, many of them painted on rocks, across fields. Path eventually ascends small hill, with wide views. Descend to gate, and 20yds (18m) beyond, take path downhill to **R** to gated stone stile on to road.

❸ Turn **R** along road. After 200yds (183m) go **R** through gate by sign 'FP to B6160'. Follow path across fields, crossing stile to reach wall. Turn **R** here,

following wall and then yellow-waymarked posts. Eventually descend to stone stile on to road.

❹ Turn **L** and walk along road for 300yds (274m), then turn **R** into car park and pass beside **Strid Wood Nature Trails Kiosk**. Follow paths ('The Strid') down to river bank; turn **R** to reach narrowest part of river at **The Strid**.

❺ From **The Strid**, continue on riverside path until you reach information board and gateway near **Cavendish Pavilion**. Go through gate, turn **L** by café and go over footbridge.

❻ Immediately at end of the bridge turn **R** ('**Bolton Abbey**'). Follow path parallel with river, eventually descending to bridge beside stepping-stones and **priory**.

❼ Cross bridge and walk straight ahead up slope and steps to gateway – known as the Hole in the Wall. Go through gateway then keep ahead beside green to reach car park.

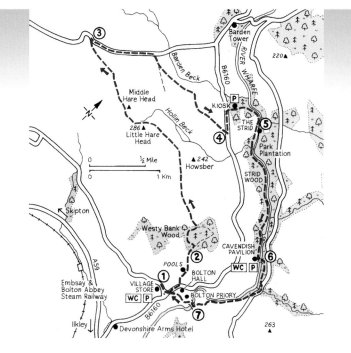

Kendal Two Castles

3 miles (4.8km) 1hr 30min **Ascent:** 300ft (91m)
Paths: Pavements, surfaced and grassy paths with steps, no stiles
Suggested map: OS Explorer OL7 The English Lakes (SE)
Grid reference: SD 518928
Parking: Free parking area by river (occasionally occupied by fairground), plenty of pay car parks near by

Visit two ancient castles.

❶ Walk upstream along riverside parking area to footbridge. Cross and bear **L** to follow surfaced walkway, through **Gooseholme**. At junction of roads by **Church of St George** turn **R** down Castle Street. Pass **Castle Inn** and join Ann Street. Turn **R**; continue up hill to **Castle Road** on **R**. Ascend **Castle Road** to where kissing gate on **R** leads on to Castle Hill. Follow broad path ascending shoulder to **Kendal Castle**.

❷ Round castle ruins until, beneath its southern end, you find path dropping down to **R**. Descend steeply to pass through iron kissing gate on to Sunnyside Road. Follow Sunnyside, which becomes Parr Street; exit on to **Aynam Road**.

❸ Turn **R** along Aynam Road to crossing. Cross footbridge over **River Kent**. Bear **L**, downstream, and walk short distance to narrow, surfaced path leading **R**. Continue along path, lined by yew trees and limestone coping stones, to pass between parish church and **Abbot Hall Art Gallery**. Emerge on to Kirkland Road by church gates with **Ring O'Bells** pub to L. Turn **R** along road; continue for 300yds (274m) to crossing. Cross it; bear **R** to cross **Gillingate Road** and keep along main road, now called Highgate. At chemist shop go **L** up **Captain French Lane** for 300yds (274m). Go **R** up Garth Heads Lane. Follow this until steep path ascends to **L**. Steps lead to terrace and view over Kendal. Cross grass terrace towards mound and its distinct bodkin-shaped obelisk. Climb steps then spiral **L** until, as path levels, steps lead up **R** to obelisk and top of **Castle Howe**.

❹ Return to path and go **R**. Find gap on **L** and emerge on road at top of Beast Banks. Descend hill, which becomes Allhallows Lane, to traffic lights and pedestrian crossing opposite **Town Hall**. Cross road and go **L**, then immediately turn **R** down Lowther Street. Go **L** at bottom to zebra crossing beyond Holy Trinity of St George, which leads to riverside.

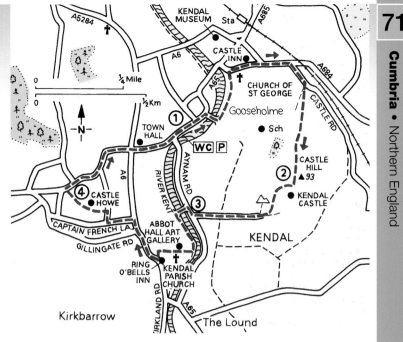

Sedgwick The Lancaster Canal

5½ miles (8.8km) 2hrs 30min **Ascent:** 600ft (183m)
Paths: Field paths, tow paths and some quiet lanes, 10 stiles
Suggested map: OS Explorer OL7 The English Lakes (SE)
Grid reference: SD 513870
Parking: Roadside parking in Sedgwick

Walking by the Lancaster Canal.

❶ From canal aqueduct, follow Natland lane as far as 2nd junction and turn **R**. At **Crosscrake church**, go **R** again ('Stainton Cross').

❷ Leave through 1st gate on **L**; cross to stile in far **R** corner of field. Follow **L-H** hedge, continuing over 2nd stile. Beyond crest, drop to **Skettlegill Farm**, cross **Stainton Beck**; walk out to lane beyond.

❸ Cross to gate opposite then pass through another gate ahead. Climb again to stile, and maintain your direction across next field. Over another stile, walk to far wall and turn **R** to corner before emerging on to track by **Summerlands**.

❹ Walk ahead, passing through gate by Eskrigg Wood. Your way shortly broadens into meadow, but keep going to further of 2 gates at **L** corner. Waymark confirms route along hedged track into rough woodland. Soon path bends **L** to stile near a gate. Walk away across field to track at far side.

❺ Follow track to **R**, leading through farmyard at **High Commonmire**, and continuing as metalled way. Bear **R** at junction and proceed to **Field End Bridge**.

❻ Cross canal, drop **L** on to tow path; walk beneath bridge. Presently, beyond aqueduct built to take waterway over **Stainton Beck**, canal ends, onward section to Kendal has been filled in, de-watered or lost beneath road construction. However, its course remains evident, eventually leading to lane below A591.

❼ Pass under bridge and rejoin canal through gate on **R**. Cutting leads to mouth of **Hincaster Tunnel**, where path to **L** carries walkers, as it once did horses, over **Tunnel Hill**. At far side, turn **R** behind cottages to regain tow path. Remain by canal until forced on to lane and continue eventually to cross A591.

❽ Beyond bridge, steps rise to field on **R**. Walk ahead by fence, shortly passing under bridge. Beyond, canal cutting is evident, accompanying you to Sedgwick, where steps beside aqueduct drop to road.

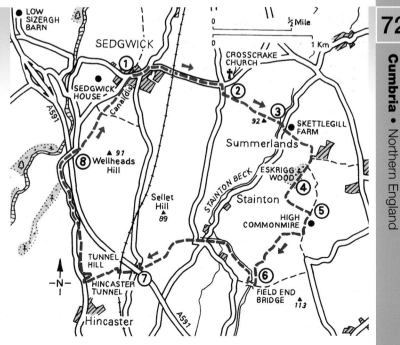

73 Pooley Bridge *A Roman Road*

4½ miles (7.2km) 2hrs **Ascent:** 740ft (225m)

Paths: Surfaced roads, stony tracks, grassy tracks and hillside

Suggested map: OS Explorer OL5 The English Lakes (NE)

Grid reference: NY 470244

Parking: Pay car parks either side of bridge

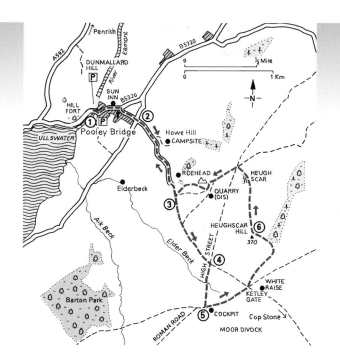

Enjoy views over the lake, cross a Roman road and spot the prehistoric artefacts.

1 From bridge over **River Eamont** follow main street (B5320) through **Pooley Bridge**. Pass church; turn **R** to follow pavement along Howtown Road.

2 At junction continue over crossroads. Road rises and becomes pleasantly tree-lined before ending at unsurfaced track beneath **Roehead**. Gate and kissing gate lead out on to open moor.

3 Go through kissing gate and climb broad track, continuing to where going levels and track intercepts route of **High Street Roman road** (signed).

4 Bear **R** along now very boggy stretch of Roman road to reach low circular ancient wall of earth and stone. This, the **Cockpit**, is the largest of the many prehistoric antiquities found on **Moor Divock**.

5 Way leads back diagonally north by shallow shake holes (sinkholes) to original track at **Ketley Gate**. (Little to R, **White Raise** burial cairn is worthy of

attention.) Either follow track (route marked on map), which leads off north ascending to walled wood high on hillside and then bear **L** to find top of **Heughscar Hill**, or go **L** up well-worn path through bracken, starting by stone parish boundary marker. Flat summit of hill offers rewarding views.

6 Proceed north along high shoulder to pass broken little limestone crag of **Heugh Scar** below to **L**. At end of scar make steep descent of grassy hillside to point where track and grassy lane of **High Street Roman** road cross each other. Descend to **L** taking track that passes under Roman road; head in general direction of **Ullswater**. Note lime kiln and little **quarry** to **L**. Continue descent to corner of stone wall marked by sycamore tree. Follow route, which falls steeply down beside stone wall and beneath trees. Bear **L** near bottom of incline and gain original track just above gate and kissing gate situated beneath **Roehead**. Return by same road back to **Pooley Bridge**.

74 Bowness-on-Windermere *Brant Fell*

3½ miles (5.7km) 1hr 15min **Ascent:** 525ft (160m)

Paths: Pavement, road, stony tracks, grassy paths, 2 stiles

Suggested map: OS Explorer OL7 The English Lakes (SE)

Grid reference: SD 398966

Parking: Fee car park on Glebe Road above Windermere lake

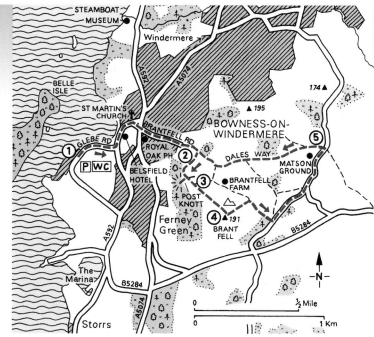

Enjoy woodlands and breathtaking views.

1 Take **Glebe Road** into **Bowness**. Swing **L** and, opposite steamer pier, go **R** over main road; turn **L**. Opposite **Church of St Martin**, turn **R** to go up St Martins Hill. Cross Kendal Road to climb **Brantfell Road** directly above. At head of road, iron gate leads to **Dales Way**, which climbs up hillside. Proceed to kissing gate by wood, leading on to lane.

2 Pass through kissing gate; turn **R** ('**Post Knott**') to follow lane. Proceed ahead, rising through woods until lane crests height near flat circular top of **Post Knott**. Bear **L**; make final short ascent to summit. Retrace steps to track; bear **R** to kissing gate, leaving wood on to open hillside.

3 Beyond kissing gate take grassy path, rising to rocky shoulder. Cross shoulder and first descend, then ascend to ladder stile in top corner of field by fir trees. Cross stile; bear **R** to ascend up open grassy flanks of **Brant Fell** to rocky summit.

4 Go **L** (north) from top of fell, descending grassy path intercepted by grassy track. Bear **R** here; follow track to stone stile and gate on to road. Turn **L** on road; continue **L** at junction to pass stone buildings and entrance drive to **Matson Ground**. Immediately beyond is kissing gate on **L**, waymarked **Dales Way**.

5 Go through kissing gate; continue down field to cross track; pass through kissing gate into another field. Keep on grassy track until path swings **L** to emerge through kissing gate on to surfaced drive. Go **R** along drive for 30yds (27m) until path veers off **L** through trees to follow fence. Iron kissing gate leads into field. Follow grassy path, first descending and then rising to iron gate in field corner. Continue to join grassy track; go through kissing gate. Cross **Brantfell Farm's** surfaced drive; keep ahead to another kissing gate leading into field. Follow path, parallel to wall, descending hill to intercept track, via kissing gate; regain Point **2**. Retrace route back to **Glebe Road**.

Ambleside Lilies and Lakes

3¼ miles (5.3km) 1hr 45min **Ascent:** 575ft (175m)

Paths: Road, paths and tracks, can be muddy in places, 3 stiles
Suggested map: OS Explorer OL7 The English Lakes (SE)
Grid reference: NY 375047
Parking: Ambleside central car park

Above little Ambleside.

❶ Take wooden footbridge from car park; go **R** along Rydal road to pass waterwheel and Bridge House. At junction bear **R** along Compston Road. Continue to next junction (cinema on corner); bear **R** to cross side road and enter Vicarage Road alongside chip shop. Pass school; enter Rothay Park. Follow main path through park to emerge by flat bridge over **Stock Ghyll Beck**. Cross beck, then go **L** to cross over stone arched **Miller Bridge** spanning **River Rothay**.

❷ Bear **R** along road over cattle grid until, in few paces, steep surfaced road rises to **L**. Climb road, which becomes unsurfaced, by buildings of **Brow Head**. At S-bend, beyond buildings, stone stile leads up and off **L**. Pass through trees to find, in few dozen paces, stone squeeze stile. Pass through; climb open hillside above. Paths are well worn and there are various possible routes. For best views keep diagonally **L**. Rising steeply at first, path levels before

rising again to ascend 1st rocky knoll. Higher, larger knoll follows and offers good views.

❸ Beyond this, way descends to **R**, dropping to well-defined path. Follow path to pass little pond before cresting rise and falling to little pocket-handkerchief **Lily Tarn** (flowers bloom late June to September). Path skirts **R** edge of tarn, roughly following crest of **Loughrigg Fell**. Gate/stile leads to base of further knoll and this is ascended to another viewpoint.

❹ Take path descending **R** to track below. Bear **R** to gate, which leads through stone wall boundary of open fell and into field. Continue to descend track, passing **old golf clubhouse** on **L**. Intercept original route just above buildings of Brow Head.

❺ Continue to cross **Miller Bridge** then, before flat bridge, bear **L** to follow track by side of **Stock Ghyll Beck**. Beyond meadows, lane through houses leads to main Rydal road. Bear **R** along road to car park beyond fire station.

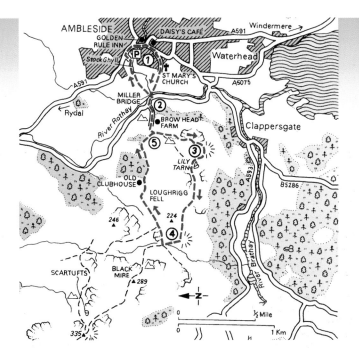

Satterthwaite Medieval Industry

4¾ miles (7.7km) 2hrs **Ascent:** 1,017ft (310m)

Paths: Mainly good paths and tracks throughout, 3 stiles
Suggested map: OS Explorer OL7 The English Lakes (SE)
Grid reference: SD 344912
Parking: Forest car park at Blind Lane

Follow paths once trodden by charcoal burners, iron smelters and coppicers.

❶ Path from back of car park, marked by green-and-white-topped posts, heads **R**, over rise to forest trail. Walk **L** and, after 400yds (366m), turn **L** on to path through birch wood. Go ahead over junction at top and descend to join metalled track into **Satterthwaite**.

❷ Turn **L** by church; walk through village. After ¼ mile (400m), at L-H bend, go **R** on to track, **Moor Lane**, and then at marker post, head **L** on to rising path into trees. Bear **L** in front of reconstructed charcoal burner's **hut** and then shortly drop down on to broader track.

❸ Go **R**, over another hill and **R** again where you eventually reach broad forest trail. Pass **waterfall**. Beyond, track bends across stream before rising to junction. Turn **L** for 220yds (201m) and branch **L** again on to unmarked, descending grass track.

❹ Emerging on to lane at bottom, go **R**, then turn in between cottages at **Force Forge**. Through gate on **R**, go **L** by tall beech hedge and across **Force Beck**. Continue along winding path into **Brewer Wood**, bearing **R** when you shortly reach crossing path.

❺ After about ¼ mile (400m), at fork, bear **L** to gap in wall and continue through trees. Reach indistinct fork beyond crest of the hill and take **R-H** branch, which descends to **Rusland** Reading Rooms. Cross out to lane in front of church and walk **L**.

❻ After little way along, leave lane for byway opposite junction. Climb over top of **Stricely** beside wooded pastures and eventually drop to lane at **Force Mills**. Go **R** and then **L** to ascend beside **Force Falls**.

❼ At green-and-white post, part-way up hill, turn **R** on to path climbing steeply into larch plantation. Keep **R** where path forks, shortly passing through gap in wall. Go through another gap few paces on; descend through trees back to car park.

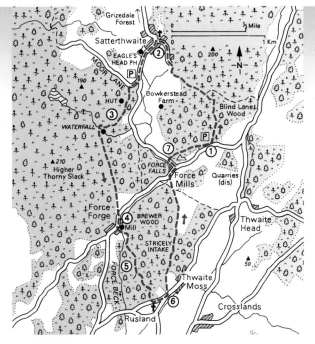

77 Elterwater Four Seasons Walk

4 miles (6.4km) 2hrs **Ascent:** 328ft (100m) 2

Paths: Grassy and stony paths and tracks, surfaced lane, 4 stiles
Suggested map: OS Explorer OL7 The English Lakes (SE)
Grid reference: NY 328048
Parking: National Trust pay-and-display car park at Elterwater village

Bluebell woods, a lake and Little Loughrigg.

❶ Pass through small gate to walk downsteam above **Great Langdale Beck**. Continue to enter mixed woods of **Rob Rash**. Gate leads through stone wall (open foot of **Elter Water** lies to R). Continue through meadows above river. (Lane can be wet and prone to flooding.) Pass through gate and enter mixed woods. Keep along path to pass **Skelwith Force** waterfall down to R. A little bridge leads across channel to viewing point above falls. Keep along path to pass through buildings (Kirkstone Quarry).

❷ **Kirkstone Gallery** is on R, as path becomes surfaced road. Continue to intercept **A593** by bridge over river. Turn **L** to pass **hotel**. At road junction cross over Great Langdale road to lane, which passes by end of cottages. Follow lane, ascending to intercept another road. Turn **R** for short distance, then **L** towards **Tarn Foot** farm. Bear **R** along track, in front of cottages. Where track splits, bear **L**. Through gate to

continue on track to overlook **Loughrigg Tarn**. At point halfway along tarn cross stile over iron railings on **L**.

❸ Follow footpath down meadow to traverse **R**, just above tarn. Footpath swings **R** to climb ladder stile over stone wall. Follow grassy track leading **R**, up hill, to gate and stile on to road. Turn **L** along road, until surfaced drive leads up to **R** ('Public Footpath Skelwith Bridge'). Pass small cottage and keep on track to pass higher cottage, **Crag Head**. Little way above this, narrow grassy footpath leads off **R**, up hillside, to gain level shoulder between outcrops of **Little Loughrigg**.

❹ Cross shoulder and descend path, passing little tarnlet to R, to intercept stone wall. Keep **L** along wall descending to find, in a few hundred paces, ladder stile leading over wall into upper woods of **Rob Rash**. Steep descent leads to road. Cross this, and go over little stone stile/broken wall next to large double gates. Descend track to meet with outward route. Bear **R** to return to **Elterwater**.

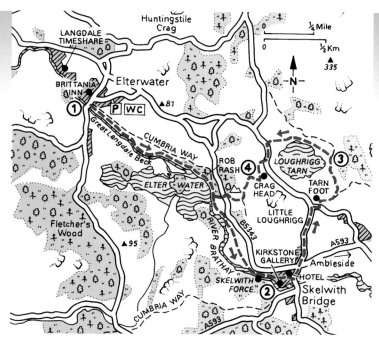

78 Stonethwaite Herries Family Saga

4½ miles (7.2km) 3hrs 30min **Ascent:** 1,102ft (336m) 3

Paths: Bridleways, fairly good paths and some rough walking
Suggested map: OS Explorer OL4 The English Lakes (NW)
Grid reference: NY 262137
Parking: By telephone box in Stonethwaite

Through Walpole's Herries country – from Stonethwaite to Rosthwaite.

❶ From parking area, turn **R** and walk down track to **Stonethwaite Bridge**. Cross it and go through gate then turn **R** on to bridleway to Grasmere. Go through another gate. After about 150yds (137m), look for path off to **L**, through gap in low wall.

❷ Follow path uphill, through wood, then cross stile and continue uphill on well-paved path through trees. Path emerges from trees still climbing. Cross stile beside **Willygrass Gill** and follow path to **Dock Tarn**.

❸ Ignore track going R, over beck, and continue on obvious path around **L** side of tarn. There are rocky sections but going isn't difficult. If lower path is flooded, there are higher paths available to your **L**, which lead in same direction.

❹ At north end of tarn broad path continues above boggy ground in direction of gap between 2 low crags. Ahead, view opens up. Just past small rock pinnacle

on L, **Watendlath** comes into view and path descends steep rocky staircase to kissing gate.

❺ Go through gate, cross beck; follow green-topped wooden posts on stone path across bog. Turn **R** at junction ('Watendlath'); descend to sheep pen. Go through gap in wall and descend to kissing gate.

❻ Go through gate, follow stream downhill, cross it then follow line of wall round field before turning **L** on to farm track. Go through 2 gates and turn **R** across old pack bridge into **Watendlath**.

❼ From Watendlath re-cross little bridge and follow public bridleway sign to **Rosthwaite**. Walk uphill on well-used route; go through kissing gate and head downhill, passing gate on R. At bottom of hill, sign on wall indicates that path continues to **Stonethwaite**.

❽ Ignore sign and instead turn **R** through gate in wall, go downhill, pass through another gate beside **Hazel Bank** hotel; turn **L** on to public bridleway and follow it to **Stonethwaite Bridge**.

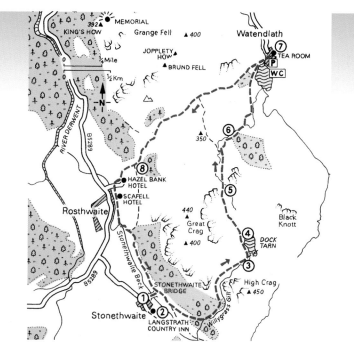

Latrigg Taking the Line

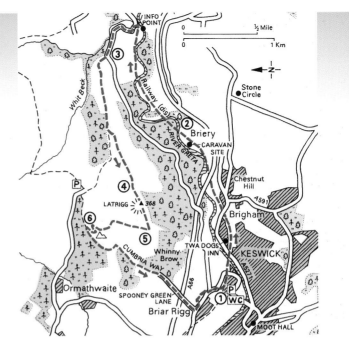

5 miles (8km) 2hrs **Ascent:** 902ft (275m)
Paths: Railway trackbed, country lane, grassy fell paths, 3 stiles
Suggested map: OS Explorer OL4 The English Lakes (NW)
Grid reference: NY 270238
Parking: At former Keswick Station

A walk along a disused railway line leads to a fine viewpoint above Keswick.

❶ From old Keswick Station, head along trackbed, away from **Keswick**. Beyond **A66** road, here cantilevered above trackbed, route covers boardwalk section high above **River Greta**, before continuing to site of bobbin mill at **Low Briery**, now **caravan site**.

❷ Beyond **Low Briery**, **River Greta** is agreeable companion as far as old railway building on R used as **information point** (with river bridge beyond) – but keep your binoculars handy. Greta's fast-flowing waters are a habitat for many young invertebrates, making it a popular hunting ground for dippers, kingfishers and grey heron. Before reaching building, turn **L** through gate and cross narrow pasture to back lane. Turn **L** and climb, steeply for short while, to reach footpath ('Skiddaw and Underscar') at gate and stile.

❸ Go over stile on to broad track, which swinging round gorse bushes then runs centrally up eastern ridge of **Latrigg**. Look back here for spectacular views of Blencathra. Shortly, you reach plantation on R. Before plantation ends, climb **L** from metal gate towards top of ridge and walk along it to gate.

❹ After gate, lovely stroll leads across top of **Latrigg**, with great views of Vale of Keswick, Dodds, Borrowdale, Newlands Valley, and, to R, Skiddaw's massive bulk.

❺ Beyond highest point of **Latrigg**, bench is perfectly placed to admire view. From here take path descending gently northwards, later dropping in zig-zags to intercept track alongside another plantation.

❻ At track, turn **L**, and then continue down to **Spooney Green Lane**, which crosses high above **A66** and runs on to meet **Briar Rigg**, back lane. At this junction, turn **L** into **Briar Rigg**, and follow lane (enclosed path on L along **Briar Rigg** makes for safer passage), until you can branch **R** at pronounced L bend to return to station car park.

Bardsea Distant Past

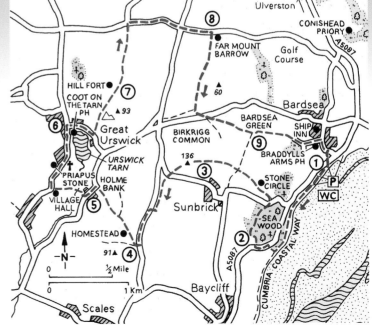

8 miles (12.9km) 3hrs **Ascent:** 577ft (176m)
Paths: Paths and tracks, some field paths may be muddy, 10 stiles
Suggested map: OS Explorer OL6 The English Lakes (SW); OL7 The English Lakes (SE)
Grid reference: SD 301742 (on Explorer OL7)
Parking: Small car parks between coast road and shore at Bardsea

A walk strewn with ancient remains.

❶ Follow shore to **Sea Wood**. Path runs parallel, turning **R** on inside edge of wood to reach road. Turn **L**, then **R** at gate into another part of wood.

❷ Turn **L** to follow path around top edge of wood, then **L** again to leave wood at gate. Cross road; follow grassy path across **Birkrigg Common**. Turn **L** to reach wall corner; walk few paces to **stone circle**. Follow any grassy path to skyline and trig point.

❸ Pass bench; take path to **R** to reach road. Cross then walk parallel to another road – common tapers out to cattle grid. Proceed on road; make sharp **R** along walled track.

❹ Cross stile at end; bear **R** past stone trough (ancient **homestead**). Keep **L** of wall to cross stile at gate. Bear **L** to take path down valley to gate. Turn **L** before gate; cross stile; follow hedgerow across slope to house. Cross stile leading down to road; turn **L** to pass farm buildings at **Holme Bank**.

❺ Turn **R** ('Public Footpath Church Road'). Cross ladder stile and footbridge; take path to **village hall** and road. Cross road; turn **R** to pass school. Pass church and shop.

❻ Turn **R** at **Coot on Tarn** to follow another road. At Clint Cottage on L and Tarn House on R, turn **L** up steep track. At 2 gates go through gate on **L**; proceed ahead, keeping R of low wall.

❼ Wall leads to gate, then keep straight on. Cross stile on **R**, other side of gate; cross stile on **L**. Walk ahead, crossing 2 stiles to reach road junction. Turn **R** to walk through crossroads to farm.

❽ Turn **R** at **Far Mount Barrow** ('Bardsea Green'). Cross stile by gate; keep **L** to cross road on **Birkrigg Common**. Turn **L** for **Bardsea Green**, along path parallel to road, then parallel to wall.

❾ At corner of wall, go through gate; follow track to road and cross dip. Turn **L** at junction into **Bardsea** then **R** at **Braddylls Arms** pub. Follow road to shore.

81 Duddon Bridge Swinside Stone Circle

6 miles (9.7km) 2hrs 30min **Ascent:** 820ft (250m)
Paths: Good paths, some can be muddy, farm roads, 6 stiles
Suggested map: OS Explorer OL6 The English Lakes (SW)
Grid reference: SD 197882
Parking: Parking space at Duddon Iron Furnace, near Duddon Bridge

Discover Swinside Stone Circle.

❶ **Duddon Iron Furnace** is on **L** of **Corney Fell road**, soon after turning from **Duddon Bridge**. Public bridleway sign points up track beside ruins. At last building, turn **L** up woodland path marked by bridleway sign hidden among brambles.

❷ Cross narrow access road; continue uphill. Turn **R** at junction of paths and keep climbing. Join track leading further up wooded slope. Go through gate in wall on **L**; follow deep, narrow path flanked by bracken, crossing low gap in thills.

❸ Turn **R** to reach gate. Go through and follow walled track. Go through next gate; turn **L**. Path running roughly parallel to tall wall passes old **quarry** near **Thwaite Yeat** farm. Path is vague on moorland slope, but look ahead to spot signpost at road junction.

❹ Turn **L** down narrow road ('Millom'); then turn **R** along farm track. It crosses dip and leads to gate ('Fenwick'). Go through; follow track almost to farm,

but turn **L**, following public footpath sign. Cross 3 stiles as path leads through fields to **Black Beck**.

❺ Cross footbridge; climb uphill, looking ahead to spot **Swinside** farm. Keep to **R** of buildings, but turn **L** to follow access road away from buildings. **Swinside Stone Circle** is in field on **L**.

❻ Walk down farm access road; continue on tarmac road to white building. Just before it there is stile and public footpath signpost. Field path and stile lead to **Black Beck** and **stepping stones** lead to **Beck Bank Farm**. Use **L** of 2 tracks, leading from farm to road

❼ Turn **L** and **L** again on busy main road. Walk to reach 2 farm roads signposted as public bridleways. Take 2nd one to **Ash House**. Narrow footpath leads away from buildings; stile leads into woods. Walk uphill, then down to reach marker post at junction.

❽ Turn **R**; walk downhill; turn **L** at junction. Keep **R** at next junction, following path of outward route. Cross narrow access road; walk to **Duddon Iron Furnace**.

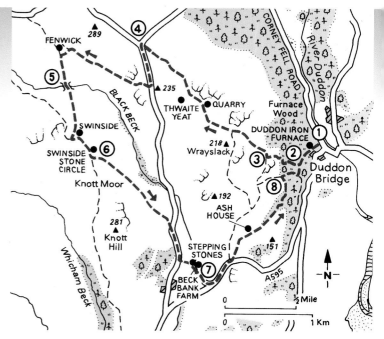

82 Buttermere In Paradise

4½ miles (7.2km) 2hrs **Ascent:** 35ft (11m)
Paths: Good path, some road walking, 2 stiles
Suggested map: OS Explorer OL4 The English Lakes (NW)
Grid reference: NY 173169
Parking: National Park car park beyond Fish Hotel (fee)

Walk through one of the Lakeland's most attractive valleys.

❶ Leave car park and turn **R**, passing **Fish Hotel** to follow broad track through gates. Ignore signposted route to Scale Force; continue along track towards edge of lake. Then follow line of hedgerow to bridge at **Buttermere Dubs**. Cross small footbridge; go through nearby gate in wall at foot of **Burtness Wood** and cascade of **Sourmilk Gill**. Turn **L** on track through woodland that roughly parallels lakeshore, finally emerging from woodland near **Horse Close**, where bridge spans **Comb Beck**.

❷ Continue along path to reach wall leading to sheepfold and gate. Go **L** through gate, cross **Warnscale Beck** and walk on to **Gatesgarth Farm**. At farm, follow signs to reach valley road. Short stretch of road walking, **L** on B5289, now follows, along which there are no pathways. Take care against approaching traffic.

❸ As road bends **L**, leave it for footpath on **L** ('Buttermere via Lakeshore Path'). Path leads into field, beyond which it never strays far from shoreline; continue to stand of Scots pine, near **Crag Wood**.

❹ Beyond Hassnesshow Beck bridge, path enters grounds of **Hassness**, where rocky path, enclosed by trees, leads to gate. Here path has been cut across crag where it plunges into lake below, and shortly disappears into brief, low and damp tunnel. The tunnel was cut by employees of George Benson – 19th-century Manchester mill owner – so that he could walk around the lake without straying too far from its shore. After you emerge from tunnel, gate gives access to gravel path across wooded pasture of **Pike Rigg**, beyond which clear path leads to traditional Lakeland bridge of slate slabs.

❺ Short way on, through gate, path leads to **Wilkinsyke Farm**, and easy walk out to road, just short way above **Bridge Hotel**. Turn **L** to return to car park.

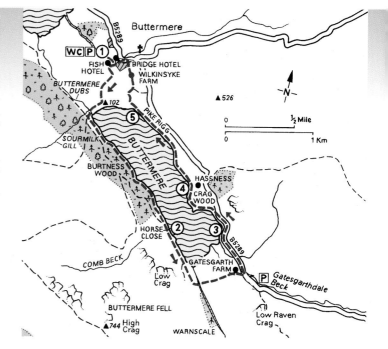

Loweswater Getting High

5 miles (8km) 3hrs Ascent: 650ft (200m)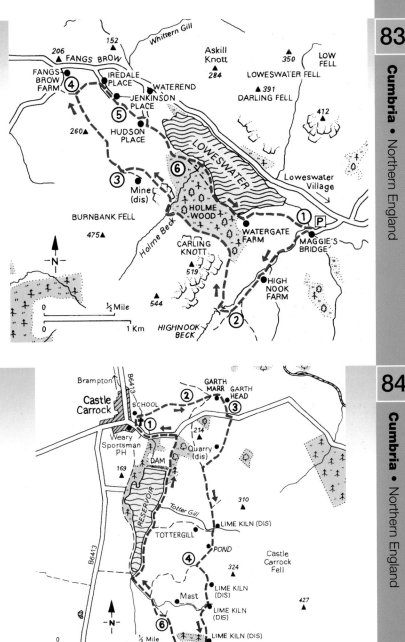

Paths: Well-defined paths and tracks, all stiles have adjacent gates

Suggested map: OS Explorer OL4 The English Lakes (NW)

Grid reference: NY 134210

Parking: Maggie's Bridge pay car park, Loweswater (get there early)

Discovering the Lakeland's finest balcony.

1 Just opposite car park entrance at **Maggie's Bridge** go through gate ('**High Nook Farm**') and follow track through fields. After passing through farmyard continue on stony track that climbs into comb of Highnook Beck and beneath **Carling Knott**.

2 Take **R** fork each time path divides. This will bring you down to footbridge across beck. Across bridge route continues as fine grassy track that doubles back **R** raking across hillside to top of **Holme Wood** plantations. Track follows top edge of woods before traversing breast of **Burnbank Fell**.

3 Track swings **L** and climbs to ladder stile and gate to north of fell. Here it divides. Ignore **L** fork, which doubles back to an old mine. Instead go over stile and descend gradually northwest across high pastureland.

4 Couple of hundred paces short of road at **Fangs Brow**, turn **R** over ladder stile and continue along rutted track past **Iredale Place farm**. Just beyond

house track joins tarmac lane.

5 On reaching **Jenkinson Place** (farm) tarmac lane ends. Turn **L** here over stile and follow well-defined grass track across fields towards **Hudson Place** and lake. Signpost diverts way **L**, around farm complex. Path meets lane from **Waterend** (farm). Turn **R** and follow lane, which nears shores of **Loweswater** before entering National Trust's **Holme Wood**. Oak predominates near the lake, although the trees at the top of the wood largely consist of pine, larch and Sitka spruce. **Holme Wood** is one of the last strongholds of the red squirrel. You're very likely to see pied and spotted flycatchers here, and maybe, if you're lucky, a green woodpecker.

6 Wide track now heads through woods, but by taking path to **L**, you can get nearer shoreline. This 2nd path rejoins original track just beyond stone built outhouse. At **Watergate Farm**, turn **L** to follow wide gravel road back to car park at **Maggie's Bridge**.

Castle Carrock Lime Kilns

4½ miles (7.2km) 2hrs Ascent: 476ft (145m)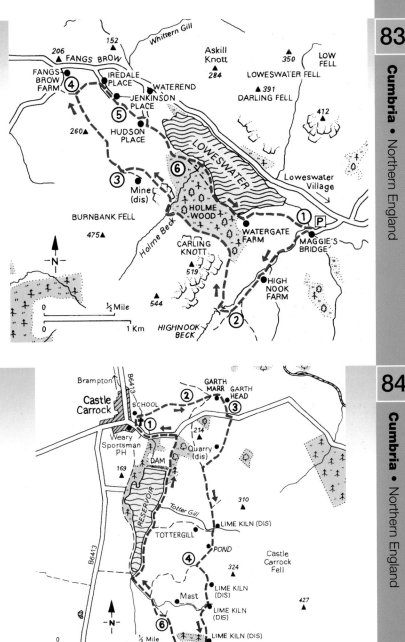

Paths: Field paths, farm tracks, metalled lanes, 7 stiles

Suggested map: OS Explorer 315 Carlisle

Grid reference: NY 543553

Parking: On street between parish church and Watson Institute

Discovering fine industrial remains.

1 Facing **church** turn **L** then **R** past school ('**Garth Head**'). Cross bridge into field by stile. Ascend **L** of hedge and maintain direction through trees up to gate on **L**. Keep hedge **R** and continue up hill, cutting corner of field. Continue with hedge **R**, up to stile in corner behind bush.

2 Bear slightly **L** up bank and across field then go through gate in top **R** corner. Follow lane through **Garth Marr** farmyard then through 2 gates by **Garth Head** farmyard. Walk up track into field, then turn **R**, up to gate on to road.

3 Go **L** for 20yds (18m) then **R** ('**Brackenthwaite**'). Walk along field edge to wall. Join track with wall on **L**. Follow until wall comes in **R**. Go through gap. Follow track with wall now **R**. After 350yds (320m) cross stile. Eventually, go through gap in wall and join track from **L**. Descend to bridge with **lime kiln** up to **L**. Continue to **L** of wall, ahead. Track leads through reeds then **L** of

pond. Cross stile on far side. Bear **R** to fingerpost.

4 Turn **L** up **R** edge of field to gate. Turn **R** alongside fence. Past **lime kiln** on **L**, path opens out and continues through gap in wall into boggy area. Keep **L** and continue along base of hillside. Cross beck and pass **lime kiln**. Continue along track following wall on **R**. Go through stile **R** and follow path with wall now **L** for 100yds (91m) to **lime kiln**.

5 Turn **R** through gap in wall. Follow track down to **L** of tin-roofed shed. Cross stile and bear **R** down track. Go through gate on to road. Turn **R**, round back of farmyard, signposted to reservoir. At corner of yard, carry on through gateway, turning **R** in front of barn to gate on **R**. Walk up track for 10yds (9m), turn **L** and cross 4 fields to gate on to road, just past green shed.

6 Turn **L**. Follow road for ½ mile (800m) to junction. Turn **R** and follow track by reservoir, ignoring turn to **Tottergill**. Pass dam and go through woods to gate on to road. Turn **L**; walk back into **Castle Carrock**.

85 Sedbergh The Quakers

4½ miles (7.2km) 1hr 30min Ascent: 131ft (40m)

Paths: Mostly on field and riverside paths, 7 stiles

Suggested map: OS Explorer OL19 Howgill Fells & Upper Eden Valley

Grid reference: SD 659921

Parking: Pay-and-display car park just off Sedbergh main street (which is one-way, from west)

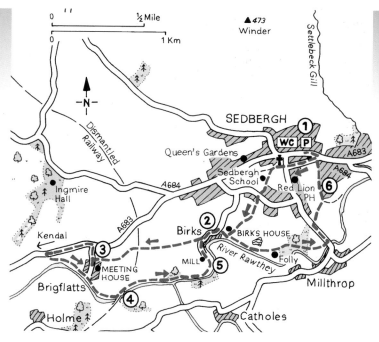

A walk to the Quaker hamlet of Brigflatts.

❶ From car park, turn **R** along main street, continue to junction with main road; turn **L**. At churchyard turn **R** ('Cattle Market or Busk Lane'). At next signpost, go **L** behind pavilion; straight ahead through 2 kissing gates and out on to road. Cross and go through another metal kissing gate ('Birks'). Follow path through another gate to **Birks House**.

❷ Go through kissing gate beyond house; turn **L** along lane. Opposite Old Barn go **R**, through metal kissing gate. Follow **Brigflatts** sign roughly half **L** to waymarker. Go through 4 gates and under gated railway arch. Continue ahead and go through, in turn, gate in crossing wall, metal kissing gate and farm gate on to lane opposite Quaker Burial Ground.

❸ Turn **L** to visit **Meeting House**, then return to gate, continuing up lane to main road. Turn **L**. Just beyond bend sign, go through signed kissing gate in hedge on **L**. Follow riverside path through 2 gates to

another gate, to **L** of large railway bridge over river.

❹ Go through gate; over embankment to another gate. Continue along riverside, passing through gate near confluence of 2 rivers, then 2 more gates to reach metalled lane by old **mill**.

❺ Follow lane back into **Birks**. Go **R**, though kissing gate ('Rawthey Way') (you went through this gate on outward route). By hedge around **Birks House**, bear **R** towards river and over stile. Follow river to another stile; climb slightly **L** to stile by gateway; past **folly**, to **L** of wood, through kissing gate. Walk through wood to stile. Go across field to metal gate then stile on to road by bridge. Turn **L**. By ('30') sign, go **R**, though stile. Go across field to another stile; bear **L** alongside building to another kissing gate.

❻ Cross drive to another kissing gate. Continue downhill to another, and go straight on along lane to main road. Cross over road. Walk behind row of houses, along **Sedbergh's** main street to car park.

86 Cowgill Along River Dee

3½ miles (5.7km) 1hr 30min Ascent: 131ft (40m)

Paths: Tracks, field and riverside paths, some roads, 17 stiles

Suggested map: OS Explorer OL2 Yorkshire Dales – Southern & Western

Grid reference: SD 742864

Parking: Parking place at Ibbeth Peril

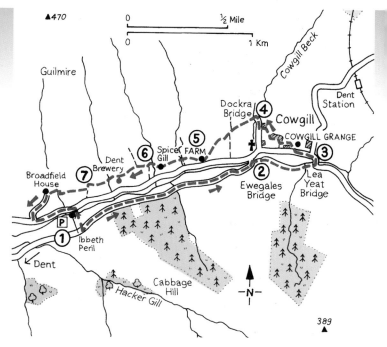

An easy walk beside the River Dee.

❶ Leave back of car park on footpath going through woodland. Cross footbridge; head across field to gate. Turn **L** along road. Follow road for 1 mile (1.6km) until stone bridge.

❷ Don't cross bridge, but continue along riverside over stile ('Lea Yeat'). Go through stone stile. Cross over 2 tributary streams to wooden stile on to **Lea Yeat Bridge**. Cross bridge; turn **L** at signpost towards Dent and Sedbergh.

❸ Just beyond post-box on L, follow sign on **R** to **Dockra Bridge**. Go short way up drive for **Cowgill Grange**; bear **L** to gated stile. Go ahead, passing through 2 gates in front of cottage and on to track. Bear **R**. Path goes round **L** end of 2 houses, through 3 gates and stile. After last gate, turn **L** to reach track; go **R** to Dockra Bridge.

❹ Cross bridge, bend **R**; take stile on **L**. Go half **L** to stile in crossing wall. Continue ahead to waymarked

handgate. Go **R** of barn, through gateway in crossing wall to another gated stone stile, then half **L** across field towards farmhouse to signposted stile.

❺ After stile go half **R** then through stile. Continue to another stile; head towards **f**arm buildings; over stone stile by gateway beside barn and through another stile. Pass farmhouse, bend **R** then bear **L** behind barn to bridge with steps and gated stile beyond.

❻ Cross field to another stile. Just beyond, turn **R** along track. As it bends **R**, go ahead to pass house, through gate and behind another building to wooden stile. Go ahead across field to stone stile, go **L** of barn on to track over stream and uphill again.

❼ Curve round **L** of next barn; follow wall. At next farm buildings, go through metal gate by barn; follow walled lane **R**. After another gate bear **L**, through stile, go to **R** of farm building and on to track. Turn **R**, then **L** through waymarked gate, pass farmhouse; follow track to road. Turn **L** to return to car park.

Causey Arch The World's Oldest Railway

4 miles (6.4km) 2hrs Ascent: 394ft (120m)

Paths: Mostly on tracks, one short stiff climb
Suggested map: OS Explorer 308 Durham & Sunderland
Grid reference: NZ 205561
Parking: Causey Arch car park, off A6076

In the footsteps of the early railway pioneers.

1 From car park, walk through 'Exit' archway, **L** of toilets. Take signed footpath, **L** of bus stop. Cross stile. Go up field to cross stile on to metalled road.

2 Turn **L**. After 200yds (184m) turn **R** ('Beamish Hall'). Where concrete track swings **R**, go straight ahead down footpath until you reach farm track. Go straight ahead. Where track forks, bend **R**. Eventually track goes through gateway and into woodland.

3 Descend between houses to road, opposite **Beamish Hall**. Turn **R**. Follow road for ½ mile (800m) to entrance, on **L**, to Beamishburn Picnic Area. Turn **L**. Follow lane through picnic site to footbridge.

4 Cross bridge. Follow footpath as it bends **R**. Where it forks, proceed by burn side. At waymarked post turn **L**, go up steps and **R** at wide crossing track to reach road. Turn **L** then go **R**, by **Mole Hill Farm** ('**Great North Forest Trail and Causey Arch**').

5 Go through wooden stile beside gate. Climb track to yellow waymark sign on post. Go **L** off track; follow path over wooden stile. Continue with hedge on **R** to another stile. Path beyond curves downhill to road.

6 Cross road; take footpath opposite. Ascend hill, cross over field and descend to another road. Turn **R**. Follow road for ½ mile (800m) to '**Tanfield Railway**' sign.

7 Turn **R**, up approach road, then go ahead through gap in fence. Follow wagon track alongside burn, above gorge. Eventually climb steps to bench by start of **Causey Arch**. To avoid descent into valley, cross arch and continue along path back to car park.

8 To view arch, turn **L** at bench and go downhill, crossing burn on footbridge. Follow path through woodland and over another footbridge. Go **R** at end, then cross another footbridge by quarry. Do not cross next footbridge, but bear **R**, up steps. Turn **L** at top. Follow embankment back to car park.

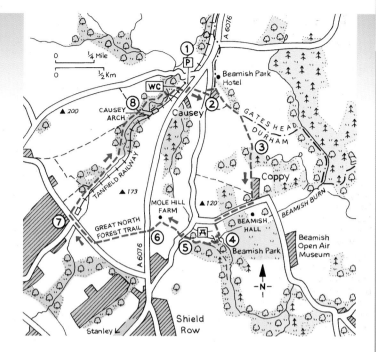

Consett A Steel Walk

3½ miles (5.7km) 1hr 30min Ascent: 311ft (95m)

Paths: River and streamside paths with some roadside walking
Suggested map: OS Explorer 307 Consett & Derwent Reservoir
Grid reference: NZ 085518
Parking: Car park off Sandy Lane, off A691

A walk along the banks of the river that first brought steel making to Consett, with plenty of industrial relics.

1 From car park, walk beside house, following wall, and then bend **R** to cross river via footbridge. Turn **L** along river bank and follow it through woodland. Where path divides, stay by river. Eventually you'll reach area of beech woodland where path rises on to wider track.

2 Follow track, keeping **L** when it forks – there are waymarks on this section. This path follows alongside wire fence, and eventually bears **R** over tiny stone bridge skirting house to reach **A68**.

3 Turn **L** down hill. Go over road bridge, passing from Northumberland into Durham. Where road joins from **L**, go **L** through entrance into **Allensford Country Park**. Bear round to **R**, and walk through grassed riverside area to car park. Go through car park to reach road by entrance to **caravan site**.

4 Go ahead across road to waymarked stile in fence opposite. Follow path, which goes up 2 sets of steps. At top follow grassy path. Where it divides, bear to **L** and follow winding path into woodland and continue downhill. When you reach crossing path by marker post, turn **L** to road.

5 Turn **R** and follow the road (take care because it can be busy). It rises through woodland and then passes through a more open area. After ½ mile (800m), pass a road off to the **R**. In ¼ mile (400m) beyond, look for a footpath that descends on your **R** to meet the road, by trees.

6 Continue ahead to follow road for 400yds (366m). As roads rises, take signed footpath **L**, downhill into woodland. The path opens out into track and then becomes path again. Follow path for ½ mile (800m) to reach lane. Turn **L** here, downhill. At bottom of hill turn **L** again, following car park sign back to start of walk.

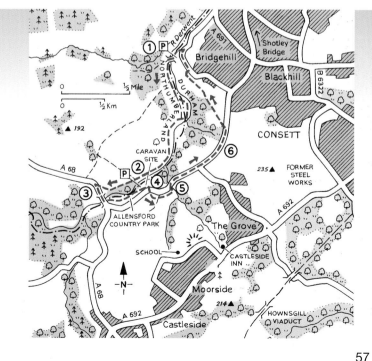

89 Westgate Through Meadow and Woodland

6¾ miles (10.9km) 4hrs Ascent: 525ft (160m)

Paths: Field paths, tracks and country lanes, 5 stiles

Suggested map: OS Explorer OL31 North Pennines

Grid reference: NY 909380

Parking: By river at Westgate

Visit Weardale's prettiest village and stride high above the land of the Prince Bishops.

1 From car park walk out to road bridge that crosses over **River Wear**. Don't cross but follow path ahead, which goes across fields alongside river's south bank. This path crosses minor road close to ford and footbridge, then continues by some cottages and across riverside meadows, passing more cottages at Windyside.

2 On reaching main road at **Daddry Shield** turn **R**, then **L**, over crash barrier and down to Wear's south bank again. This new path stays closer to river than before. Turn **L** on meeting country lane and follow it into village of **St John's Chapel**. Turn **R** along its main street and pass through village.

3 At far side of village, turn **R** along signed footpath that tucks under old railway bridge and crosses footbridge over river. Beyond crossing turn **L** through gap stile to follow path close to north bank. Ignore next

footbridge, but instead head for farmhouse, which should be rounded on **L**.

4 Follow grassy enclosed path raking diagonally across hillside pasture to reach high country lane above hamlet of **New House**.

5 Turn **R** along lane then, after about ¾ mile (1.2km), take higher **L-H** fork which traverses southern side of **Carr Brow Moor** with its disused quarries and mine shafts.

6 At its terminus turn **L** up walled **Seeingsike Road** (track). Turn **R** at junction of tracks and descend into Middlehope Cleugh. Conveniently placed stones allow you to cross over river.

7 Turn **R** again to follow **Middlehope Burn's** east bank, past series of lead mines. The path enters **Slit Woods** and comes out by mill and some cottages on outskirts of **Westgate**.

8 The lane leads to main road where you turn **L**, then **R** past **Hare and Hounds** pub, back to car park.

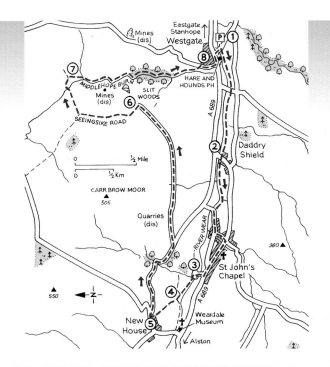

90 Barnard Castle Around old Barney

4¼ miles (6.8km) 2hrs 30min Ascent: 165ft (50m)

Paths: Town streets and good paths, 6 stiles

Suggested map: OS Explorer OL31 North Pennines

Grid reference: NZ 051163

Parking: Pay-and-display car park at end of Queen Street between Galgate and Newgate

A town and riverside walk with plenty of history.

1 From car park go through passageway signposted for river. Go across Newgate Street and continue through little ginnel, which leads through churchyard of **St Mary's**, founded in the 12th century, then out on to riverside parkland of **Demesnes**.

2 Here turn **L** along stony path, which angles down to river. It passes **Demesnes Mill** and then follows north bank of **Tees**, with river on your **R**.

3 You pass (quickly if the wind is in the wrong direction) local sewage works. Ignore upper **L** fork of 2 paths and stay by river to enter pretty woodland, which allows glimpses of remains of **Egglestone Abbey** on far banks. Go through gate on to road and turn **R** over **Abbey Bridge**.

4 Turn **R** at junction on far side of bridge, then go **L** up access track to view the 12th-century **abbey**. Return to road and follow it **L**, to pass **Bow Bridge**.

Squeeze stile in hedge on **R** marks start of path along south bank of Tees. On approach to **caravan park** path crosses fields and veers slightly away from river.

5 Turn **R** along surfaced track, down to **caravan park** and take 2nd drive on **L**, which eventually leads to continuation of riverside path.

6 Turn **R** to cross over footbridge back into **Barnard Castle** and then go straight ahead into Thorngate. Turn **L** along Bridgegate. Where road crosses County Bridge go straight ahead, on to follow path that rounds **castle** walls to entrance. The **castle** was built in 1112 for Bernard de Balliol, whose father fought side by side with William the Conqueror at the Battle of Hastings. After visiting castle continue past Methodist church to start of Galgate.

7 Turn **R** along Market Street and continue to Market Cross. Carry on down The Bank then, at top of Thorngate, go **L** to **Demesnes**. Retrace earlier footsteps back to car park.

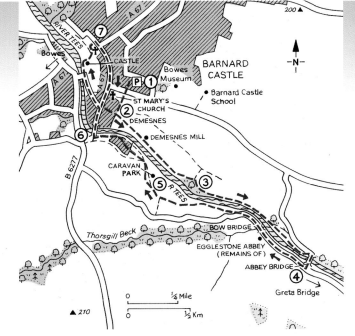

Baldersdale Wild Flowers and Moors

5½ miles (8.8km) 3hrs 15min **Ascent:** 750ft (229m)

Paths: Tracks, field and moor paths and lanes, no stiles

Suggested map: OS Explorer OL31 North Pennines

Grid reference: NY 928187

Parking: Car park by Balderhead dam

The spartan home of Hannah Hauxwell.

1 Walk across **Balderhead Dam** causeway to south side of reservoir. Double back **L** on stony track descending past **Blackton Youth Hostel**. Beyond this, grass track leads down towards **Blackton Reservoir** where it meets **Pennine Way** track beyond gate. It's worth detouring **L** from here to visit the wetlands on the northwest shores before returning to this point. Turn **R** along track and climb past **Clove Lodge**.

2 Beyond this take tarmac lane to your **L**. On your **L** you pass pastures of several farms, while on your **R** are barren slopes of **Cotherstone Moor**.

3 Just beyond driveway of **East Friar House** take path climbing half **R** (southeast) towards rocks of **Goldsborough** (part of Bowes Loop Pennine Way).

4 By 1st of rocks take **L** fork to climb to summit. Return to this position then take narrow **R** fork path that descends northwards, back to road. Turn **R** along road and follow it down to **Hury Reservoir**.

5 Just beyond **Willoughby Hall**, double back **L** along Northumbrian Water access track, then turn **R** off it along grassy causeway to north of reservoir. A path veers **L** above north shore, climbs above **Blackton Dam** where it goes through gate on **R**.

6 Once through 2nd gate in northwest corner of field, path veers **R** alongside line of hawthorns, then turns **L** beside more hawthorn trees. Past barn, walls to **R** then to **L** guide route to footbridge across **Blind Beck**. Waymarking arrows now aid route finding.

7 Footpath now·crosses 2 fields, parallel with reservoir's shoreline. In 3rd field, follow dry-stone wall half **L** down towards **Low Birk Hat**, then pass in front of farmhouse to reach stony track. House itself is now in private ownership and it is courteous not to pause too long here. Turn **R** along gated track and climb out of valley, past Hannah's Meadow and **High Birk Hat** to reach higher road. Turn **L** then take next turning on **L**, tarmac lane back to car park.

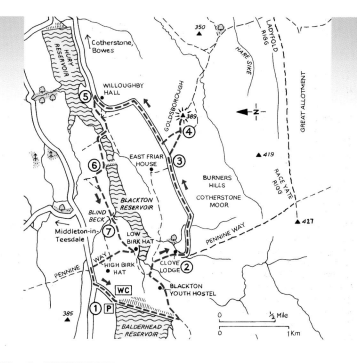

Marsden Bay Smugglers and the Light

5½ miles (8.8km) 2hrs **Ascent:** 246ft (75m)

Paths: Roads, tracks, field and coastal paths

Suggested map: OS Explorer 316 Newcastle upon Tyne

Grid reference: NZ 412635

Parking: Whitburn Coastal Park car park, signed off A183 (southern end)

Along the coast then inland to the hills.

1 Leave car park at its southern end, following gravel track toward houses. Path winds and goes past sign for Whitburn Point Nature Reserve. Follow track ahead to go through gap in wall. Turn **R**. Path bends **R**, **L** and **R** again to join road into houses. Keep ahead to join main road.

2 Cross road; turn **L**. Walk until you reach **windmill**. Turn **R** to enter grounds. Go up slope on path then between houses. Bear **L** then **R** to T-junction.

3 Keep ahead on path that goes to **R** of house No 99. When you reach another road turn **L**. Just after 1st bungalow on R, turn **R** along signed track. Follow track towards farm. Go through farmyard over 2 stiles and follow lane beyond, with hedge to your **R**; where it ends, turn **R** over stile.

4 Follow path along field edge. Cross another stile, gradually ascending. Path bends **L** then **R**, still following field edge. Go over another 2 stiles. Path will bring you to tower of **Cleadon Windmill**.

5 Go to **R** of windmill, following wall on your **R**. Go **R** through kissing gate, then bear slightly **R** (brick tower to L). Go parallel with wall on your **R**. Cross track and go through wire mesh fence at **R** angles to wall. Follow path through scrubland to emerge by yellow post by **golf course**.

6 Cross course, following yellow posts (watch out for golfers). Go over stone stile; turn **R** along signed footpath, following wall on your **R**. Path eventually descends beside houses to road.

7 Cross and take footpath almost opposite, to **R** of **caravan site**, heading towards sea. Carefully cross busy **A183** then turn **R**, following sea edge. **Marsden Rock** is near by, and **Marsden Grotto** to your **L** as you cross road. Follow coast as it bends **L** to **Lizard Point**. After visit to **Souter Lighthouse**, continue ahead on path slightly inland from coast, which returns you to car park.

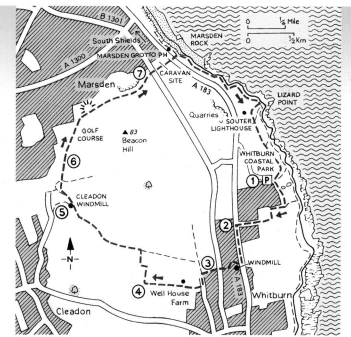

93 Chopwell Derwent Valley's Past

7 miles (11.3km) 2hrs 30min **Ascent:** 541ft (165m)

Paths: Tracks, field paths and old railway line

Suggested map: OS Explorer 307 Consett & Derwent Reservoir

Grid reference: NZ122579

Parking: Roadside parking in Chopwell; follow signs for 'Chopwell Park Car Park' (irregular opening)

Steel making and Roman remains.

❶ Walk up entrance road to Chopwell Park. Turn **R** past barrier; bear **R**, past sign 'Chopwell Woodland Park'. Follow woodland track, turning **R** at crossing track. Pass barrier to metalled area. Turn **R**. Follow track downhill. Where woodland ends cross stile and continue on fenced path. Enter farmyard through gate.

❷ Bear **R** and follow track to road in **Blackhall Mill**. Turn **L**, over bridge. Just after footpath sign, go **L** along field edge, **R** of hedge. Follow riverside path. At crossing path, turn **L**, uphill. At top go sharp **L**, following waymark signs. Go **L** of buildings, over stile and across field. Go over 2 stiles; turn **R**. Follow track uphill, passing **Derwentcote Ironworks**, to main road.

❸ Cross and take signed footpath almost opposite. Go over stile and, at crossing path, turn **R** to another stile. Follow path through woodland to former railway track. Turn **R**; follow track, which crosses another track (barriers at each side) and eventually rises to

another barrier on to metalled lane.

❹ Turn **R** and descend into **Ebchester**. Bend **R** by community centre to meet main road. Cross and turn **R** in front of **post office**. Turn **L** at footpath sign beyond. Follow fence on your **L**, bend **L** at end beside wall then follow footpath downhill to reach metalled lane. Turn **R** along lane to footbridge.

❺ Cross bridge. Footpath bends **R** before going straight ahead across field to stile. Follow green lane uphill, pass **farmhouse** and follow track through 2 gates. Where main track bears **L**, keep ahead. Go through farm gate, and along field edge. Go through 2 gates to T-junction of tracks.

❻ Turn **L** ('Whinney Leas'). About 300yds (274m) after farm go **R**, over stile; walk across field to another stile, hidden in hedge. Continue up field to stile **R** of houses, and along narrow lane. At end, turn **R** along tarmac lane. At main road turn **R** then **L**, following 'Chopwell Park Car Park' signs back to your car.

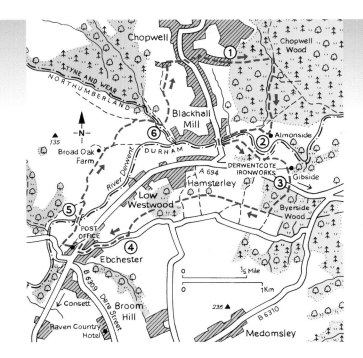

94 Norham The Tweed Valley

4½ miles (7.2km) 1hr 30min **Ascent:** 205ft (62m)

Paths: Field and woodland paths, 4 stiles

Suggested map: OS Explorer 339 Kelso & Coldstream

Grid reference: NT 899473

Parking: Roadside parking in Norham

A delightful wander along the Tweed, returning past Norham's former railway station and ancient castle.

❶ Leave village green by cross, heading along Pedwell Way to **St Cuthbert's Church**. In churchyard, walk along grassy path between graves to pass behind north side of church, where you will find stile, which marks head of enclosed path down to **Tweed**. Follow river bank upstream, shortly arriving at **Ladykirk** and Norham Bridge.

❷ Immediately beyond, go over ladder stile on **L**, turn **R** and continue at field edge. Towards its far end, approaching **Bow Well Farm**, look for stile, which takes path down tree-clad bank and out to lane. Walk **R** and, at end, pass through gate ('Twizell Bridge') to carry on across pasture in front of cottage and then through 2nd gate into wood. An undulating path continues above river.

❸ When you reach path junction by footbridge, go **L**

through broken gate. Bear **L** again a little further on and climb to another junction at top of wood. Now turn **R** to walk above **Newbiggin Dean**, passing beneath stone arch of railway viaduct. Shortly, at fork beyond stile, take **R** branch ('East Biggin'), which eventually leads out on to lane.

❹ Turn **L**, climbing over hill to descend between piers of dismantled railway bridge. Just before here, to **L**, is former **Norham Station**, which closed in 1964. Its buildings are now restored and house railway museum. Continue to walk on to end of lane.

❺ Turn **R**, but then leave some 250yds (229m) further on, through opening on **L**, signed as bridleway to **Norham Castle**. Keep ahead along field edge to bottom corner, where gated track continues beside brook through trees. Shortly, go **L** over bridge into field, and there turn **R**, following its edge out to lane. Turn **L** and walk past entrance of **Norham Castle**, eventually returning to village.

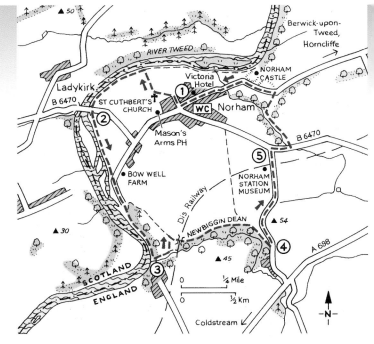

Kirknewton Ancient Yeavering Bell

5 miles (8km) 2hrs 15min Ascent: 1,115ft (340m) **3**
Paths: Tracks, field paths and moorland, steep ascent and descent
Suggested map: OS Explorer OL16 The Cheviot Hills
Grid reference: NT 914302
Parking: In Kirknewton village, in wide area of road beyond school and church, off B6351

Views of the Cheviot Hills and the sea are the reward for climbing to this hilltop fort.

1 From parking place, walk towards village centre; turn **L**. Just before gate, bend **R** along lane, following 'Hillforts Trail' sign. Metalled lane bends **R** again and becomes grassy track. Go through metal gate and ahead at next waymarker. Go through 2 metal gates and gateway. At next marker post bear **R** ('Permissive Path') and go over stream and ladder stile.

2 Turn **L** after stile then cross another stile. Bear half **R** across field to handgate in crossing wall. Go through gate, and bear **R** to reach waymarked post beside track. This is part of **St Cuthbert's Way**.

3 Turn **L** along track and follow it through wooden waymarked gate, past farmhouse and over cattle grid. Just before next cattle grid turn **R** off track, following 'St Cuthbert's Way' sign. Bend **L** through gate and continue along grassy track uphill to ladder stile in wall on your **L**.

4 Go over stile and turn **R** to follow footpath uphill. At low-level signpost, turn **L** ('Yeavering Bell'). Follow waymarks down into valley, across stream then uphill. Path eventually passes through fort wall. Bend **R** to reach summit of **Yeavering Bell**.

5 After enjoying view, go downhill to valley between 2 peaks. Bear **R** and head downhill, on opposite side of hill to that which you came up. Go through wall and follow waymark just beyond. Path is waymarked all the way down steep hill, until you reach stile.

6 Go over stile then ladder stile on your **R** on to track. Follow track past marker post and, just after it, bend **L** towards another track, which leads towards farm buildings in valley bottom. Go over ladder stile by buildings. Turn **R** along track. Go through metal gate and past cottages to reach road.

7 Turn **L** along road and follow it back to **Kirknewton**. At 'Yetholm' sign at entrance to village keep ahead, through gate, then turn **R** back to start.

Breamish Valley Burned Hamlets

5 miles (8km) 2hrs 30min (add another hour for detours) Ascent: 590ft (180m) **2**
Paths: Part metalled road, part hill tracks, 1 stile
Suggested map: OS Explorer OL16 The Cheviot Hills
Grid reference: NT 976162
Parking: Roadside parking at Hartside

The remains of an ancient settlement.

1 From parking place, **Hartside**, take metalled road ('Alnhammoor') over cattle grid then turn sharp **R** and go downhill. At bottom of hill, road turns **L** and leads to wooden bridge. Cross bridge and continue steadily uphill, past farm and across 3 more cattle grids.

2 Near top of 1st rise, another track joins main roadway from **L**. You are now on side of **Meggrim's Knowe**. (A relatively easy but trackless detour over hill to **R** and down to shoulder on other side, about ¼ mile (400m), to remains of Celtic **settlement**.) Continue on metalled road, passing small wood on **R**, and over next rise to reach dip in road. At bottom, turn **R** on to prominent grassy track that leads downhill to valley floor and footbridge over river.

3 Cross footbridge and low stile. Turn **L** along track, passing **waterfall** after 220yds (201m). Continue across open stretch of land, lined along river bank with copper beeches, go through gate and uphill past new

oak and rowan woodland. Gate gives access to open hillside. A few hundred paces after this, track becomes grassy and can be swampy in places. Continue for further ¼ mile (400m) to join track leading from **L**. Turn **R** along this to another track and again go **R** to fence.

4 Go through gate and down to side of forest, passing through another gate on way. **Linhope Spout** can be reached by following lower track along forest edge, through kissing gate and downhill for ¼ mile (400m). Back on main route, follow rubble track to **R** to reach **Linhope** after ¼ mile (400m).

5 Metalled road leads across bridge and uphill for 220yds (200m) to where broad track on **L** gives into field at side of forest. To visit **Grieve's Ash**, go on to this track then follow edge of forest steeply uphill for 110yds (100m). The extensive remains of the settlement occupy the area behind the forest. Main road leads you back to **Hartside** in ½ mile (800m).

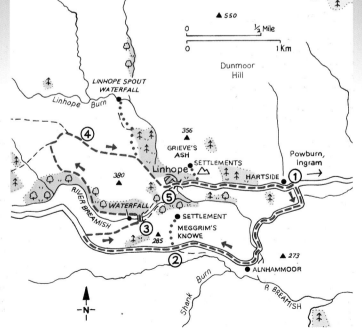

Craster A Ruined Castle

5 miles (8km) 1hr 45min Ascent: 275ft (84m)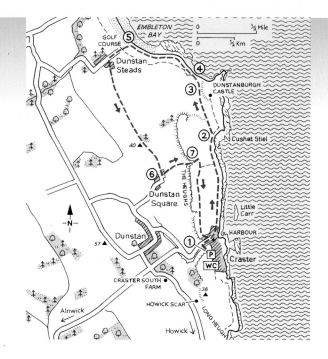

Paths: Generally good tracks, some field paths tussocky, 1 stile

Suggested map: OS Explorer 332 Alnwick & Amble

Grid reference: NU 256198

Parking: Pay-and-display behind Craster tourist information centre

The castle that inspired artist JMW Turner.

❶ From car park, turn **R** towards village. Immediately before **harbour**, go **L** into Dunstanburgh Road ('Castle') and continue through gate at end above rocky shore towards **Dunstanburgh Castle**.

❷ After 2 more gates, if you want to visit castle, keep to main track, which leads to its entrance. Otherwise, bear **L** on less distinct path through gorge on landward side. Continue below castle, with ruins of Lilburn Tower, perched on top of rocky spur outcrop.

❸ Beyond, as you pass above bouldery beach, glance back to cliffs protecting Dunstanburgh Castle's northern aspect, which, in the early summer, echo to the screams of seabirds, squabbling for nesting sites.

❹ Go through kissing gate at edge of **golf course**, bear **R** to remain above shore. Ahead is **Embleton Bay**; if tide permits, continue along beach.

❺ Shortly, look for prominent break in dunes, through which path leads across **golf course** to meet lane. Follow it up to **Dunstan Steads**, turning **L** immediately before on to drive ('**Dunstan Square**'). Where this bends behind buildings, bear **L** across open area to gate and continue over open fields on farm track.

❻ After 1 mile (1.6km), at **Dunstan Square**, pass through 2 successive gates by barn and turn **L** through 3rd gate ('Craster'). Walk down field edge and through gate at bottom then along track rising through break in cliffs ahead, **The Heughs**. Keep going across top to field corner and turn through gate on **R**.

❼ Walk away, initially beside **L-H** boundary, but after 150yds (137m), by gate, bear **R** to follow line of ridge higher up. Eventually meeting corner of wall, continue ahead beside it. Shortly after crossing track, go on over stile, beyond which path becomes more enclosed. Approaching village, path turns abruptly **L** behind house and emerges on to street. Follow it down to main lane and turn **R**, back to car park.

Simonside Hills Ancient Spirit

5½ miles (8.8km) 3hrs Ascent: 820ft (250m)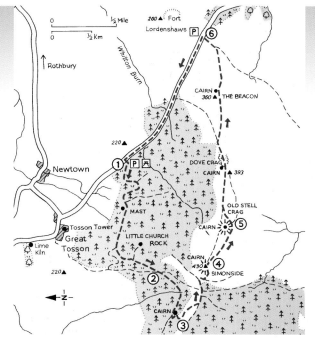

Paths: Generally good tracks, but steep and muddy in places

Suggested map: OS Explorer OL42 Kielder Water & Forest

Grid reference: NZ 037997

Parking: Large car park at forest picnic area

A hill that had spiritual significance to early settlers and now popular with rock climbers.

❶ From notice board in picnic area, go through gate on to broad forest road. Follow this gently uphill, swinging to **R** round long hairpin bend, then back **L** at top of hill. When road splits, take **R-H** fork, past communications **mast** and go gently downhill. When you get to next junction, take **L-H** fork and follow road past sign indicating detour to **Little Church Rock**.

❷ When you come to marker post, where narrow track leads to L, ignore this and continue along broad track, which now becomes grassy. After passing huge, heavily overgrown boulder, continue to small **cairn** which marks start of subsidiary track on **L**. Follow this track uphill through forest and out on to heather-covered hillside. You will now see **Simonside's** crags ½ mile (800m) away to your **L**.

❸ Continue up narrow track to join broader one at edge of upper forest and follow this for about 275yds (251m) to corner of trees. A rough track, sometimes quite muddy in places, picks its way through boulders up the hillside. Follow this, keeping crags on your L-H side, on to plateau and walk along top of crags to large **cairn** on the summit, which is probably a burial mound, built around 350 BC.

❹ Away from summit, track splits into 2. Follow **R** fork across boggy ground for ⅓ mile (530m). Climb short rise, keeping wonderfully wind-sculpted **Old Stell Crag** to your **L**. and move round on to summit and another large **cairn**.

❺ Take narrow path down to join lower track. This leads, in ½ mile (800m), to **cairn** on **Dove Crag**. At Y-junction, ¼ mile (400m) further on, follow **R** fork gently uphill to **The Beacon** cairn, and continue downhill for ½ mile (800m) to join road at **Lordenshaws** car park.

❻ Turn **L** and follow road for 1 mile (1.6km) until you arrive back at forest picnic area.

Corbridge Romans and Countryfolk

6 miles (9.7km) 3hrs 30min Ascent: 525ft (160m) ⚠
Paths: Village streets, riverside and farm paths and lanes, 8 stiles
Suggested map: OS Explorer OL43 Hadrian's Wall
Grid reference: NY 992642 Parking: On town centre streets

Discover Corbridge, Catherine Cookson's home and a rich history.

❶ Start at Low Hall Pele on eastern end of Main Street. Head west down Main Street. Turn **R** up Princes Street. At town hall turn **L** along Hill Street, then, just before church, turn **L** up narrow street to pass Vicar's Pele. Turn **R** at Market Place; head north up Watling Street, then Stagshaw Road, which is staggered to **L** beyond Wheatsheaf Inn.

❷ Go **L** along Trinity Terrace then **L** again along footpath ('West Green'). This leads past Catherine Cookson's old house, Town Barns, to Orchard Vale. Here, turn **R**, then **L** along lane to river.

❸ Turn **L** along Carelgate. Follow riverside path to town bridge. Cross bridge; follow south banks of Tyne on unsurfaced track that passes cricket ground at **Tynedale Park** before mounting grassy embankment running parallel to river.

❹ Turn **R** up steps, cross ladder stile, then railway tracks (with care). Another stile and steps lead through wood and across field to **A695**; turn **R** – footpath on nearside.

❺ Just beyond cottages, turn **L** up lane, which zig-zags up **Prospect Hill**. Just after 1st bend leave lane for southbound path that climbs fields. Just before woods, path meets track; turn **R** for few paces to rejoin lane. continue to crossroads at top of hill; turn **R**.

❻ After passing **Temperley Grange and West farms** leave road for path on **R** that follows first R-H side, then L-H side of dry-stone wall across high fields and down to **Snokoehill Plantations**.

❼ Go through gate to enter wood. Turn **L** along track running along top edge. Track doubles back to **R**, soon to follow bottom edge of woods.

❽ Turn **R** beyond gate above **High Town** farm; follow track, which becomes tarred beyond **West Fell**.

❾ Beyond **Roecliff Lodge** path on L crosses field to reach **A695**. Cross, then continue into copse, The Scrogs, before joining B6529 by Corbridge Railway Station. Follow this over bridge and into **Corbridge**.

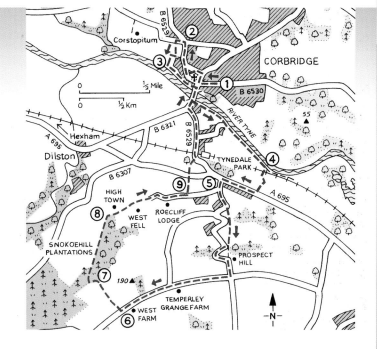

Hexham An Historic Town

3¾ miles (6km) 2hrs Ascent: 590ft (180m) ⚠
Paths: Town streets, lanes and woodland paths, 4 stiles
Suggested map: OS Explorer OL43 Hadrian's Wall
Grid reference: NY 939641
Parking: Pay-and-display car park, next to supermarket

A walk round the abbey and market town.

❶ From car park (not supermarket end) take exit between tourist information centre and café to follow narrow street past Old Gaol. Go under arches of Moot Hall and enter Market Place. Take tour of The Sele, park grounds surrounding **Hexham Abbey**, before aiming roughly southwest across them to Queen Hall on Beaumont Street.

❷ Turn **R** along here to reach Benson's Monument then continue straight ahead on unnamed street. After taking 1st turning on **R** ignore Elvaston Road on L, but instead go straight ahead on tarred lane that leads to foot of wooded Cowgarth Dene.

❸ At bridge, turn into woodland where unsurfaced track crosses footbridge and climbs out to little park at edge of modern housing estate. Follow woodland edge, then track past water treatment works.

❹ On nearing housing estate, go through gate on **L** then double-back **L** on path by houses. Where path turns **R**, climb steps on to track that runs along north side of **Wydon Burn Reservoir**, filled with reeds and tall grasses, not water.

❺ Turn **L** along lane then, at **Intake** farm, turn **R** along path that leads into thick woodland of **Wydon Burn's** upper reaches. A narrow path continues through woods to reach lane at Causey Hill where you turn **L** past campsite to junction with road, **The Yarridge**. The modern building you'll see here is part of the **Hexham Racecourse**.

❻ Turn **L** along road and go ahead at crossroads.

❼ Beyond **Black House**, stile on L marks start of downhill, cross-field path into **Hexham**. Beyond step stile path veers **R** to round gorse bushes before resuming its course alongside **L** field edge.

❽ Just before reaching whitewashed cottage go over stile on **L** and follow road down into town. Turn **L** along shopping street at bottom, then **R** along St Mary's Chare, back to Market Place.

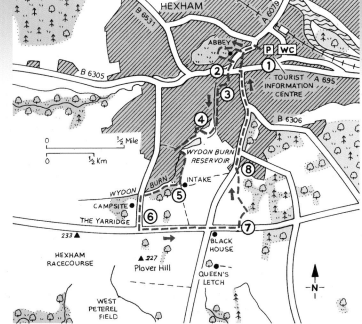

Walking in Safety

All these walks are suitable for any reasonably fit person, but less experienced walkers should try the easier walks first. Route finding is usually straightforward, but you will find that an Ordnance Survey map is a useful addition to the route maps and descriptions.

Risks

Although each walk has been researched with a view to minimising the risks to the walkers who follow its route, no walk in the countryside can be considered to be completely free from risk. Walking in the outdoors will always require a degree of common sense and judgement to ensure that it is as safe as possible.

- Be particularly careful on cliff paths and in upland terrain, where the consequences of a slip can be very serious.

- Remember to check tidal conditions before walking along the seashore.

- Some sections of route are by, or cross roads. Take care and remember traffic is a danger even on minor country lanes.

- Be careful around farmyard machinery and livestock, especially if you have children or a dog with you.

- Be aware of the consequences of changes of weather and check the forecast before you set off. Carry spare clothing and a torch if you are walking in the winter months. Remember that the weather can change very quickly at any time of the year, and in moorland and heathland areas, mist and fog can make route finding much harder. Don't set out in these conditions unless you are confident of your navigation skills in poor visibility. In summer remember to take account of the heat and sun; wear a hat and carry spare water.

- On walks away from centres of population you should carry a whistle and survival bag. If you do have an accident requiring the emergency services, make a note of your position as accurately as possible and dial 999.

Equipment

- The most important single item of equipment for country walking is a good pair of sturdy boots or walking shoes. Boots give better support to your ankles, especially in rough or hill country, and your feet need to be kept warm and dry in all conditions.

- Britain's climate is unpredictable, so warm and waterproof clothing is the next essential, but you don't need to spend a fortune on an Everest-specification jacket for a gentle stroll. There are many efficient and breathable alternatives which need not cost the earth. Waterproof trousers or gaiters are also a good idea and, as up to 40 per cent of body heat is lost through the head, a warm hat is essential.

- None of the walks in this book will take more than a day, but you will need a rucksack to hold extra clothing, food and drink for the longer walks. Look for one with about a 20 to 35-litre capacity, with stormproof pockets for your map, compass (a good ideal on any hill walk), camera and other bits and pieces.